CORVETTE

The Definitive Guide to the All-American Sports Car

ANDREW MONTGOMERY

THUNDER BAY
P·R·E·S·S

San Diego, California

To C. P. Stokes Esq.

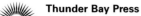

Thunder Bay Press
An imprint of the Advantage Publishers Group
THUNDER BAY 5880 Oberlin Drive, San Diego, CA 92121-4794
P · R · E · S · S www.thunderbaybooks.com

Published by Salamander Books, The Chrysalis Building, Bramley Road,
London W10 6SP, England

© Salamander Books, 2003, 2005

An imprint of **Chrysalis** Books Group plc

All notations of errors or omissions should be addressed to Thunder Bay Press, Editorial Department, at the
above address. All other correspondence (author inquiries, permissions) concerning the content of this book
should be addressed to Salamander Books Ltd. at the above address.

ISBN-13: 978-1-59223–513-1
ISBN-10: 1-59223-513-1

The Library of Congress has cataloged the original hardcover edition as follows:

Montgomery, Andrew, 1952–
    Corvette : the definitive guide to the all-American sports car / Andrew Montgomery.
      p. cm.
    Includes index.
    ISBN 1-59223-061-X
    1. Corvette automobile–History. I. Title.

  TL215.C6M65 2003
  629.222'2-dc21   2003050734

Printed in China
1 2 3 4 5   09 08 07 06 05

Credits
Commissioning Editor: Marie Clayton
Design and Layout: Hardlines Ltd, Charlbury, Oxford, U.K.
Picture Research: Andrew Montgomery
Reproduction: Anorax

Picture Credits
All pictures Copyright © Chrysalis Images except for the following:

James Mann: 16-17, 174, 178-9, 180-1, 212-3, 214-5, 216-7, 220-1, 232-3, 234-5, 236-7, 258-9, 260-1, 265, 266-7, 272-3, 284-5, 292-3, 298-9, 300-1, 308-9, 310, 312-3, 314-5, 316-7, 342, 388-9, 404-5, 406-7, 408-9, 410-1, 414-5, 416, 418-9, 420-1, 423, 425, 426, 430, 433, 435, 436-7, 438-9, 440-1, 442-3, 447, 449, 453, 454-5, 456-7, 459, 461, 462-3, 464-5, 466-7, 472

Classic & Sports Car magazine, London: 16

By kind permission of the Chevrolet Division of General Motors: 8-9, 468-9, 470-1, 472-3, 474-5

© AFP / Getty Images: 483
© GM Media Archive, 2004: 476, 477, 478, 479, 480, 481, 482

Contents

Introduction

sports car
n (1928): a low small usu. 2-passenger automobile designed for quick response, easy maneuverability, and high-speed driving

That's what it is, according to Merriam-Webster's Collegiate Dictionary. The date that the term first appeared—1928—indicates that it is most probably European in origin. In 1928, supercharged Bentleys and Mercedes-Benzes were racing at Brooklands and Le Mans, along with Bugattis and Alfa Romeos. Sports cars were being produced in every country in Europe while in the United States, Errett Lobban Cord was just about to unveil the superb, front-wheel-drive L-29 to fill the gap between his attractive and attractively priced Auburns, and his magnificent and monumentally expensive Duesenbergs. The legendary Stutz Blackhawk was ready to go into production; the stage was set for America to take on the world with home-produced performance cars that would equal and surpass anything built in Britain, Italy, France, or Germany—but the Great Depression intervened. In the lean and hungry years of the 1930s, many of the greatest names in the American automobile industry passed into history and folklore, Cord, Auburn, Duesenberg, and Stutz among them. The stock market collapse of 1929 delayed the idea of a true sports car being designed and built in the United States for a generation, but the babies born into the tumult that followed the Wall Street crash would, by the time they reached their twenties, be able to enjoy a period of unparalleled American prosperity while much of Europe was reduced to rubble and its people were still reeling from the horrors of the Second World War.

It was in 1927, a year before the term "sports car" was first coined, that the man who, more than any other, was responsible for giving America her very own sports car, joined the General Motors Corporation. During his long reign as head of GM's styling studio—originally called the "Art and Color Section"—Harley Earl oversaw the design of over fifty million vehicles. Many of these have achieved iconic status: the Buick Roadmaster, the Cadillac Eldorado, and the Tri-Chevys. "Mister Earl," often derided for his bullying behavior and his fondness for fins and chrome, may well be judged by history to have been the most influential car designer of the twentieth century. Earl's bold, innovative, uncompromising, all-American approach to automobile styling can be summed up in one car, in one word: Corvette.

For half a century the Corvette has been acknowledged to be America's first and foremost performance car—the original and best. The Corvette may justly be described as the flagship of the mighty General Motors Corporation, the largest producer of automobiles in the world. During its fifty years of continuous production, this car has embodied the

Left: Chevrolet Corvette, 1953: truck motor, bus tires, and two-speed transmisson; one of the greatest automotive stories ever told starts here.

Below: You've come a long way, baby. The latest generation of Corvettes are among the most technologically advanced automobiles in the world, but they remain true to their proud and unique heritage.

Far Right: One of the most enviable positions on the road: the driver's seat of a Corvette.

changing tastes of the American driver but has remained, at all times, an object of desire to which millions aspire. Despite its shaky first steps, the Corvette has consistently managed to outperform the most glamorous offerings of companies like Aston Martin, Porsche, and Ferrari. Even after the considerable price increases of the latest, supersophisticated generation, the 'Vette still offers a lot more bangs per buck than the products of Newport Pagnell, Stuttgart, or Maranello. The adherence of the Corvette's engineers and designers down the years to the sound, simple, robust, and reliable basic principles preferred by American drivers has produced a car that can deliver gut-wrenching performance without stomach-turning running costs or constant maintenance headaches. Owning and driving a Corvette is, for an American, at once a patriotic statement and a demonstration of good sense.

1953–1955
The Grand Original

In the beginning

In the austere years immediately following the end of the Second World War, everybody was ready for some fun, and none more than the British, who would continue to endure rationing until well into the 1950s. American servicemen based in England were able to sample one of the earliest manifestations of postwar festivity in the shape of the MG sports car. William Richard Morris, later to become Lord Nuffield, was the Henry Ford of the British automobile industry. Morris Garages had produced their first sports car in 1923 and the postwar TC was in the classic mold: crude and cramped, with a simple, ladder-frame chassis and a tiny, 1,250 cc motor, but it was a whole lot of fun for a guy to drive and the kind of car that girls liked to be driven in. It was about youth

Below: The inspiration for the styling of the first generation of Corvettes was an unlikely mixture of traditional English sports cars like the MG TD and Harley Earl's love affair with airplane design.

low, squat feel of the car was further enhanced by the wide front and rear tracks: 57 and 59 inches, respectively. Not only did this package enable the car to look good, it also provided the basis for good handling. The motor would be placed three inches closer to the ground than on any previous Chevrolet model, setting the center of gravity low. It was also set much farther back than was common practice, being a full seven inches closer to the passenger compartment bulkhead. This provided near-perfect weight distribution: not quite 50/50, but close enough at a time when a lot of American cars carried their motors almost over the front axle, a weight distribution of 53/47, front to rear.

McLean's decision to adopt a chassis with box-section side members, stiffened with a solid cross member, meant that it would be impossible to adapt an existing chassis. The rear suspension incorporated a Hotchkiss

Right: Ed Cole breathed new life into the aged Stovebolt Straight-Six, raising output from 115 to 150 bhp.

drive system instead of Chevy's standard Torque-Tube. The leaf springs were located outboard of the chassis members in an attempt to improve high-speed stability. The cost of all this made it imperative that the maximum number of existing parts be used elsewhere in the design in order to keep the costs within the brief. Front suspension was therefore provided by standard parallel wishbones and coils from a Chevrolet saloon, upgraded and given an antiroll bar. The drum brakes were standard-issue Chevy, with the master cylinders enlarged to give the pedal more feel. Steering was via a recirculating ball system from GM-Saginaw. The transmission, which would come in for much adverse comment, was Chevrolet's tried and trusted, two-speed Powerglide unit.

Ed Cole's search for a motor worthy of a true sports car was pretty fruitless. The only engine that would fit the chassis, if not the bill, was a prewar unit intended for use in trucks, the 235 cu. in. Stovebolt Straight-Six. This unit was extremely tough and reliable but was designed to be low-revving, which was hardly what was required. Ed Cole managed to increase output from 115 bhp at 3,600 rpm to 150 bhp at 4,500 rpm. Torque climbed from 204 lb. ft. at 2,000 rpm to 223 lb. ft. at 2,400 rpm. This was achieved by the introduction of a high-lift, long-dwell camshaft, utilizing mechanical tappets in place of the hydraulic originals, along with

Below: Harley Earl himself owned a curvaceous and elegant Jaguar XK120, and its lines undoubtedly influenced early Corvette styling.

dual-rate valve springs. An aluminum dual-intake manifold was adopted, the cylinder head was subtly modified, and the compression ration raised from 7.5:1 to 8.0:1. The cooling system was improved and a triple set of Carter YH carburetors was fitted, using side drafts in order to fit below the low hood line. The big, four-blade fan was accommodated by lowering the water pump; even the front of the rocker cover had to be shaved off to fit. Theoretically, the car was capable of around 110 mph.

The interior was given a faintly European flavor, drawing on the Jaguar XK120 for inspiration: bucket seats and a central instrument binnacle. The exterior was totally original and distinctive. The car looked long and low, its slab sides relieved by chrome rubbing strips. The headlights were blended into the bodywork and equipped with integral wire stone guards, while the rear lights, in a flash of aeronautical inspiration, were set in embryonic fins that had fins of their own. Bumpers were relegated to the status of ornament, consisting of delicate chrome units fixed to the fenders. The wraparound windshield echoed a fighter plane design as well, and the radiator grille, with its thirteen gleaming chromium teeth, was unquestionably aggressive. The car had a suitably masculine, muscular, almost predatory look. It was a stunner, and the decision was made to go into production. The car was to be

Below: Despite its European inspiration, the 1953 Corvette was instantly identifiable as *the* American sports car.

Above & Right: The venerable "Stovebolt Six" was a Chevrolet truck motor dating from 1927, hardly sporting but effectively indestructible. Ed Cole's boys managed to raise horsepower from 115 bhp to 150, allowing a three-figure top speed.

named after a small, fast, maneuverable warship that had distinguished itself in the Second World War: The Corvette was born.

The eager crowds who swarmed into the grand ballroom of New York's Waldorf-Astoria Hotel in January 1953 were completely bowled over at the sight of Chevrolet's amazing offering. The Corvette, finished in Polo White with a bright red interior, was displayed on a revolving turntable against a silvered photograph of the Manhattan skyline. As the great *Motorama* caravan traveled on to Chicago, Dallas, Kansas City, Miami, Los Angeles, and San Francisco, over four million people came to gaze—but how many of them would buy?

SPECIFICATIONS

1953
Wheelbase 102"
Length 13' 11"
Width 5' 10"
Weight 2,850 lb.
Transmission 2-speed auto
Brakes 11" drum
Engine 235 V-6
Compression 8.0
Gross Horsepower 150

Left: Earl's brief glimpse of the Lockheed P-38 influenced a generation of American Automobiles.

Above: The 1953 chassis mainly used existing production components.

Left: The constrictive convertible top dropped into a storage space, and was covered by a hinged deck lid panel.

Opposite: The 1953 Corvette's styling details were unique and instantly recognizable. The wire stone guards were later deleted as they didn't meet regulations in some states and were considered too "feminine."

Below: Whatever the origins of its styling, the Corvette looked, as it still does, like an all-American automobile.

Keen to capitalize on the incredible success of the Corvette's *Motorama* debut, General Motors management decreed that production should commence in June 1953. This was exactly a year after chassis and engine work had begun and a mere six months after the first model had been unveiled as a "design exercise." Despite the apparent impossibility of the deadline, the first production Corvette rolled off the line at Flint, Michigan, on June 30, 1953, but right from the start the Corvette suffered from a what might be termed a conflict of interest. The term "sports car" was generally accepted as indicating that a car had racetrack performance, along with the noise and discomfort that that usually entailed. In order to make the new model appealing to the wider American public, who were used to being cocooned and cosseted rather than getting shaken, rattled, and rolled, the Corvette offered "comfort and convenience," causing it to fall woefully short of the expectations of many sports car enthusiasts, while its sporting

pretensions alienated it from those who regarded it as an attractive, boulevard cruiser. In this regard, the crude, clip-on side curtains with Plexiglas windows were a major turnoff. Not only was this arrangement drafty and prone to leaks, it had to be penetrated, when the hood was erected, in order to get into the car, as there were no exterior door handles. This was not the kind of thing to create a favorable impression on the kind of girls that a 1953 Corvette buyer might reasonably be expecting to impress.

The two-speed transmission was hardly likely to appeal to those who craved the seat-of-the-pants driving experience of an MG and the engine lacked punch. Tuning the triple carburetors was a delicate task and would result in either smooth idling or crisp throttle response, but not both; similarly, they could be adjusted to allow the motor to run sweetly in either hot or cold temperatures, but not both. The brakes still lacked feel and were alarmingly prone to fade, while the handling was rather less than taut.

Left & Previous Page: Full of youth, vigor, freedom, and confidence, the 1953 Corvette is a symbolic summation of postwar America.

Previous Page: The hood was not the original Corvette's strong point, either in terms of style or practicality.

Right: The crossed-flag motif has graced the Corvette for half a century and remains as desirable a badge as any.

Opposite: Panel fit was a problem on early cars, as was the fitting of the awkward, canvas side-screens.

To cap it all, or rather to end it all, it was discovered that, by some strange, aerodynamic twist of fate, exhaust gases were sucked back in the slipstream to stain the white bodywork. For a while consideration was given to forming the Corvette's bodywork out of alloy, but the cost factor weighed in favor of sticking with GRP.

The final sticker price was $3,490, $1,000 more than an MG and a little under $1,000 less than the Jaguar XK120, which was considered distinctly upscale. The success of the Corvette's introduction at *Motorama* encouraged the belief that as many as 20,000 cars might be sold annually, but it was decided, wisely, that it might be better to start out with more modest goals, particularly as volume production of GRP panels was unknown territory. The target for 1953 was a mere 300 cars, all of them Polo White. The following year it was hoped to produce—and sell—10,000.

The original Corvette assembly line was a mere six cars long, tucked away in a corner of the massive Chevrolet plant at Flint. The engines had to be brought in from the factory in Tonawanda, New York, while the

The epitome of elegance: The line of the 1954 *Motorama* hardtop was a great improvement on the canvas hood but it wasn't offered until 1956, on a radically revised Corvette.

forty-six pieces that made up the body were produced by the Molded Fiber Glass Company of Ashtabula, Ohio. To begin with, inevitably, production was painfully slow and final quality extremely variable. By the time production was shifted to a purpose-built plant in St. Louis, Missouri, in 1954, a mere three cars a day were being completed. By the middle of that year, this figure had risen to six hundred cars a month, with a choice of colors: Polo White with red interior, Pennant Blue Metallic with tan interior, and Sportsman Red with red and white interior. A very small number, probably about half a dozen, were painted black and had a red interior. The cars came with 6.70 x 15 whitewall tires, a recirculating, hot-water heater, and a Delco signal-seeking radio. Instrumentation included a clock and a tachometer that read to 5,000 rpm. Output was moving steadily up to a target of a thousand a month when it was realized that supply was outstripping demand.

The high price had put the Corvette out of reach of the youthful market at which it was aimed. To try to rectify this, the 1954 model was marked down to $2,774. Potential customers lured by the attractive new price were surprised to discover that the only transmission available was listed as an option, as were the windshield wipers and the heater. The true price was, in fact, $3,250. Road testers agreed that the Corvette was neither a racer nor a cruiser. Production was halted at 3,640 and by the end of the year nearly 1,500 of those were still sitting in dealers' showrooms.

1954 also saw the birth of Ford's Thunderbird, which would go on sale the following year. This was also a two-seater, and based on an identical, 102-in. wheelbase. It was described, enigmatically, as a "personal car" and offered, from the outset, a V-8 engine and a choice of either manual or automatic transmission. The T-Bird was far more luxuriously appointed than the Corvette but still managed, at $2,994, to undercut its "real" price substantially. Ford had planned their new model meticulously, having conducted market research over a period of years. The Thunderbird was produced in big numbers from the outset, and Ford's confidence was not misplaced. In the first full year of production, 16,155 Thunderbirds were sold against a measly 700 Corvettes. GM had already decided to continue production and the arrival of this upstart from their archenemy served only to stiffen their resolve to make the Corvette the car it really wanted to be. The arrival of another inspired engineer, this time from Europe, would help to rectify the situation. Zora Arkus-Duntov set to work, trying to fix the exhaust blow-back problem and the poor handling. Chief engineer Ed Cole picked up a project from

Right: For all its much-publicized shortcomings, the 1953 Corvette remains a handsome and purposeful car.

Below: The rear aspect is as clean-cut and uncluttered as the front, though the exhaust tended to stain the pure white bodywork.

his predecessor, E. H. Kelley, in the shape of the now legendary small-block V-8. Originally intended to have a capacity of 231 cu. in.—smaller than what was officially termed the "Blue Flame Six" fitted in the Corvette—Cole had the capacity increased to 265 cu. in. He also reworked the cylinder heads, concentrating on efficient gas flow and better combustion. The V-8 was 300 lb. lighter than the Stovebolt and a remarkably compact unit, with lightweight valve-gear and much thinner cylinder walls and water jacket than was current Detroit practice. A short-stroke crankshaft allowed the engine to rev to 6,000 rpm.

In its standard state of tune, as fitted to Chevrolet sedans, this engine would produce up to 170 bhp. When employed in the Corvette, it was fitted with a four-barrel carburetor and dual exhausts and produced 195 bhp at 5,000 rpm. Maximum torque was 260 lb. ft. at 3,000 rpm. This brought the 0–60 mph acceleration time down from eleven seconds to under nine. Styling revision was limited to an oversize, gold *V* in "CheVrolet," as inscribed on the front fenders, and a broadening of the radiator grille. There were still no roll-up windows or exterior door handles and sales remained low at 674, but 99 percent of buyers were opting for the V-8 motor.

Opposite & Below: The calm before the storm. The styling of the first Corvette reflects the residual restraint of the early 1950s, just before the dawn of the rock and roll era.

Left: *Motorama* 1954 showcased a Corvette-derived station wagon, the Nomad, and a fastback coupe bearing the doomed title of Corvair. The hardtop in the foreground would appear on the restyled models of 1956.

Above: Initial sales were slow, but Chevrolet did their best to bring the product to the people with the Corvette Cavalcade, seen here traversing Chicago's Lake Shore Drive.

Left: The Corvette Cavalcade makes its merry way along the Los Angeles Harbor Freeway.

This Page: The 1954 *Motorama* Corvair never went into production. A decade later, GM must have wished that the car that eventually bore the name hadn't, either.

Following Page: In addition to Polo White, 1954 Corvette buyers could have their cars finished in hot Sportsman Red or this cool Pennant Blue.

Right & Following Page:
The plate says it all, or
most of it. 1955 brought
a 265-cid, V-8 motor,
three-speed manual
transmission, and a top
speed of close to 120 mph.
Note the enlarged *V* in
"CheVrolet" on the front
fender, indicating the
new V-8 engine.

Above: Styling revision is a constant process. Here, louvers in the front fenders on a 1955 show car anticipate the gills of the 1968 Mako.

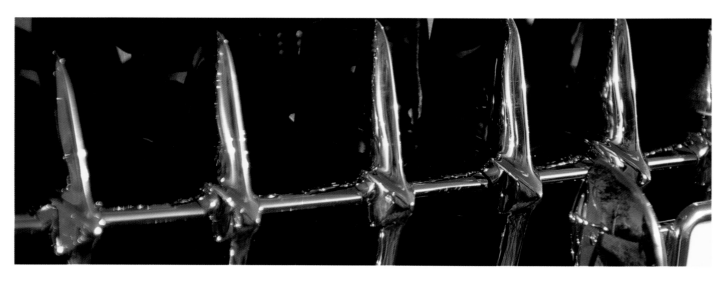

Previous Page & Right:
Earl's styling on the first-generation Corvette may not have been 100 percent ergonomic, but the overall effect is one of perfect unanimity and concord.

1956–1957
The Fuelies

To compliment the new V-8 power plant, the Corvette's body was radically restyled for 1956. Still constructed in fiberglass, this would be the last model to be designed in Detroit before the design department was relocated to GM's new technical center at Warren, Michigan. The styling was based on an amalgam of *Motorama* show cars from 1955: the Chevrolet Biscayne and a pair of designs known as LaSalle II. The Biscayne featured an interior color-keyed to its paint job, with parking lights in the fenders and a grille composed of vertical bars. The LaSalles—a roadster and a coupe—featured a detail that would become the distinguishing feature of the second-generation Corvette: the cove. This was a tapered, concave depression in the body sides that curved back from the front wheel arches into the doors. It was described as echoing the LeBaron sweep, an allusion to the coach-built automobiles of the 1920s and 1930s. The cove was outlined in chrome and usually painted in a contrasting color. The effect was magnificent; the restyled 1956 Corvette was a superb-looking automobile. The wire stone guards on the headlights were abandoned, having been discovered to be illegal in some states; the rear lights were blended neatly into the fenders and the body shape was subtly reworked to give a more purposeful appearance. The spinners on the hubcaps were still phony, as were the intake scoops that sprouted from the front fenders just ahead of the doors, but overall

Left: The restyled body of 1956 was ravishing, combining modernity and classicism in a perfectly balanced package.

Below: The signature fender "coves" recalled the coach-building of the interwar period. This detail was dubbed the "LeBaron sweep."

the improvement was huge. Beneath the surface, Ed Cole continued to push ahead with mechanical improvements. The two-speed, Powerglide transmission passed away, unmourned, to be replaced by a standard three-speed manual shift. Performance was now truly in the sports car class; the Corvette went as well as it looked, at last. Duntov had been at work on the camshaft profiles and this, coupled with a four-barrel carburetor and a compression ratio of 9.25:1, boosted output to 225 bhp at 5,200 rpm, with 270 lb. ft. of torque at 3,600 rpm. The clutch was beefed up to cope with the increased power and the rear axle ratio set at 3.55:1, with 3.27:1 as an option. In standard form, with the three-speed box, a 1956 Corvette could record a 0–60 time of around seven and a half seconds and run a standing quarter in sixteen, with a terminal speed in excess of 90 mph. Top speed was close to 120 mph.

Left: 1956: The radiator is reassuringly familiar, the rest is refreshingly different.

SPECIFICATIONS

1956
Wheelbase 102"
Length 14' 0"
Width 5' 11"
Weight 2,970 lb.
Transmission 2-speed auto
   or 3-speed manual
Brakes 11" drum
Engines
   Base 265 V-8
   Compression 8.0
   Gross Horsepower 210

   Option 469 265 V-8
   Compression 9.25
   Gross Horsepower 225

   Option 449 265 V-8
   Compression 9.25
   Gross Horsepower 240

Above Left: Seat design was beautifully integrated with the external body shape.

Above Right: The new 1956 steering wheel, unique to Corvette.

Above & Below: Whitewall tires were selected by the majority of buyers.

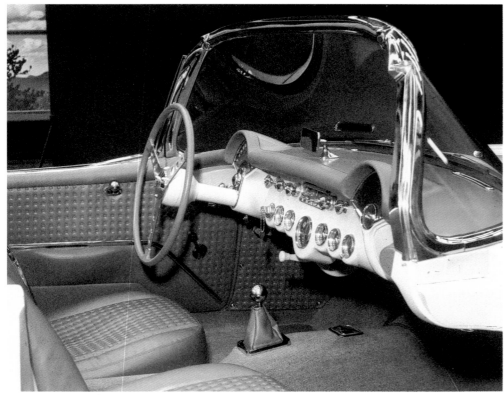

Top: This full-scale prototype is fitted with the optional hardtop, first glimpsed on *Motorama* cars back in 1954.

Right: The instrument layout is still rather haphazard, but at least there are now roll-up windows.

Despite ongoing concerns over brake fade and understeer, the Corvette's road manners were becoming more civilized. Weight distribution was now 52/48, front to rear, and the steering geared to three and a half turns, lock to lock. The price was pegged at $3,170 and there was an optional hardtop, based on a 1954 show model, plus a transistor radio— for 1956 was the year of rock and roll, notably via Alan Freed and CBS. The range of colors now available included Polo White, Onyx Black, Venetian Red, Cascade Green, Shoreline Beige, and Silver. Best of all, there were roll-up windows! Production went from under 700 to 3,467.

Just as Harley Earl and Ed Cole had put their heart and soul into the Corvette project, and laid their reputations on the line for that grand original, the plastic bathtub of 1953, so Zora Arkus-Duntov, who came to GM in that very year at the tender age of 43, was to follow suit. The Corvette became his pride and his passion and he played with it, magnificently, for twenty years. Duntov had been born in Belgium in 1909 and educated in Petrograd (formerly St. Petersburg, subsequently Leningrad, and eventually St. Petersburg again) until the Russian revolution, when the family returned to Germany, where he earned a

Below: The hood line is now much neater but somehow the car looks strangely unfinished without the outlining of the side coves.

degree in mechanical engineering. The Duntovs had to move again, this time to Paris, to escape the menace of the rise of the Nazis in Germany. In the 1930s, Duntov made a name for himself as an expert in supercharging but he also had a profitable sideline: gold smuggling. The technique was to conceal coins in the axle sleeve of a Ford V-8 and drive, under cover of darkness, for the Belgian border. On long, downhill stretches, the twenty-year-old motor would rev to around 6,000 and then run out of steam. Duntov designed an overhead valve conversion that doubled the engine's output. On arrival in the United States, he and his brother, Yura, established Ardun Mechanical in Brooklyn and put the conversion, known as the Ardun Head, into production. In the immediate postwar years he worked as a consultant to both Porsche and Mercedes-Benz in Germany and to Allard, which used Cadillac engines, in England. By late 1952 he was back in America and in the spring of the following year, just before the first production Corvette rolled off the line at Flint, he had finally arrived where he belonged—in the bosom of General Motors.

Duntov was a keen and accomplished racing driver. He took class wins in the Le Mans 24 Hours Race in 1954 and 1955, driving a Porsche Spyder! In 1956 he managed to total a hardtop Corvette at the Milford proving ground, cracking one of his vertebrae in the process. This was around the time when Harry Barr, who had succeeded Cole as chief engineer at Chevrolet, was trying, with great difficulty, to perfect the Ramjet fuel-injection system for the Corvette. Duntov was obviously the man to solve the problem, but he was immobilized by a plaster cast that held his entire upper body rigid—he couldn't even put a pair of pants on. Such was the spell that the Corvette cast, however, over all those who came into intimate contact with it, that Duntov came back to work, where, for three months, he had to stand at his desk wearing a skirt.

Ramjet was developed by Rochester Carburetor but was an in-house, General Motors design. The inlet manifold was formed in aluminum and fuel was carefully metered via a high-pressure pump that was driven direct from the distributor.

The fuel-injection option was only available on 1957's new 283 cu. in. V-8. With the Ramjet, this engine achieved the elusive one horsepower per cubic inch output in a volume-production unit that had been the goal of auto engineers for decades. The system suffered from a lot of problems in the early days, notably due to dirt getting into the fuel lines—probably from the fuel itself—and uneven running due to the injectors getting

Left: 1957 brought optional Ramjet fuel-injection, with appropriate badging to distinguish the cars so equipped.

Below: Ramjet was effective—when it worked. Early setups were notoriously temperamental.

overheated. Of the 6,339 Corvettes built in 1957, a mere 240 were fitted with the Ramjet system, but this gave them performance that was, especially in the 1950s, nothing short of awesome. An optional four-on-the-floor gear shift was introduced at a mere $188 extra. The four-speed gear box, designed by Chevrolet and built by Borg-Warner, had its additional gear interposed between first and second on the three speed, thus producing a "close-ratio" box of the kind beloved by enthusiastic drivers. Coupled to a Ramjet-equipped V-8 and driving through the optional 4.11:1 rear axle, the Corvette could hit 60 mph in 5.7 seconds, 100 mph in a little under 17 seconds, and cover a quarter mile from a standing start in 14.3 seconds, reaching a speed of 96 mph. Top speed was 132 mph.

Top Left: The 283-cid V-8 was new for 1957. Output, without fuel injection, was still an impressive 220 bhp.

Duntov realized that this second-generation Corvette would need some serious revision in the suspension, braking, and steering departments to deal with all those extra horses. His efforts finally resulted in the introduction of the Regular Production Option (RPO) 684 suspension package. This included a front antiroll bar, upgraded springs and shock absorbers, ceramic/metallic brake linings in finned and ventilated drums, Positraction limited-slip differential, and a steering modification that reduced lock-to-lock turns from 3.7 to 2.9. There were three rear axle ratio options: 3.70:1, 4.11:1, and 4.56:1. With all the goodies, the 1957 Corvette was effectively a street-legal race car. To demonstrate this, a pair of production models were the first GT-class cars to finish at Sebring that year, in 12th and 15th places. The 12th-place car finished no less than twenty laps ahead of the top-placed Mercedes-Benz 300SL, which had been, up to that point, "regarded as the world's fastest road car."

Top Right: Handsome is as handsome does. By 1957 it was hard to tell whether the Corvette went as well as it looked or looked as good as it went.

The Sebring victory was a watershed for the Corvette. It had earned the respect of the most critical of judges and had been proven in competition. In 1956, the Corvette finished first in the Sports Car Club of America's production car championship, and again in 1957. The Corvette's future was assured, even though it was still to show a profit for Chevrolet. Sadly, no sooner had the Corvette shown its ability to dominate the racetrack than General Motors signed the Automobile Manufacturers Association agreement to withdraw official support from motor racing. This was due to pressure from the National Safety Council, which claimed that using recognizable road cars on the track and referring to their race-bred qualities in advertising material had a detrimental effect on the behavior of the purchasers of such cars on the public highway. No manufacturer wanted to be seen promoting reckless driving, and so support for competition was totally withdrawn. The effect of this enforced shift of emphasis was to become noticeable in the Corvette's evolution over the next few years.

Exclusive and exciting, the 1957 Corvette offered the best of both worlds.

Right: The Corvette was campaigned competitively throughout the 1950s with spectacular success. The experimental SR-2 was constantly revised for greater performance.

Next Page: Suave, sophisticated, sporting, and sexy. The 1957 Corvette just about had it all.

1958–1962
More Chrome—More Horses

The overwhelming success of the Corvette as a race car during the 1957 season caused Ford to finally throw in the towel and make the Thunderbird a full four-seater in 1958.

Ironically, withdrawal from racing shifted the focus of the Corvette's development from "go" to "show." Harley Earl was now approaching the end of his long and distinguished career at GM and would finish with a flourish that was typical of the man: the towering, 42-inch fins of the 1959 Cadillac. The Corvette received a dose of jukebox style as well, though it didn't suit it quite so much. Quad headlights were introduced, along with a heavier grille and liberal applications of chrome, notably to the rear, where accent lines ran up from the inner edges of the back bumper and across the deck lid. Dummy louvers appeared on the bonnet, along with nonfunctional air intakes behind the heavy front bumpers and phony vents in the side coves, embellished with yet more chrome accents. Chrome strips also ran back from the headlights, along the top of the front fenders. The 1958 model rode the same wheelbase as the 1957 but was 2.3 in. wider and nearly 10 in. longer. All this added was weight, which went, at the very least, from 2,730 lb. to 2,793 lb.—63 lb. of excess fat that could, with options, rise to nearly 200 lb. This was after the car had actually gotten lighter, down from 2,764 lb. in 1956.

Left: The chrome embellishments on the 1958 Corvette were more of an imposition than an improvement.

Below: The new, improved dash panel layout is very clearly visible in this 1958 interior mock-up.

One of the few improvements, at the request of Duntov, was an overhaul of the dashboard layout that grouped all the instruments in front of the driver in a binnacle, rather than having them spread, impressively but illegibly, across the width of the fascia. Driver and passenger got the benefit of seat belts as standard and the passenger got a grab handle as

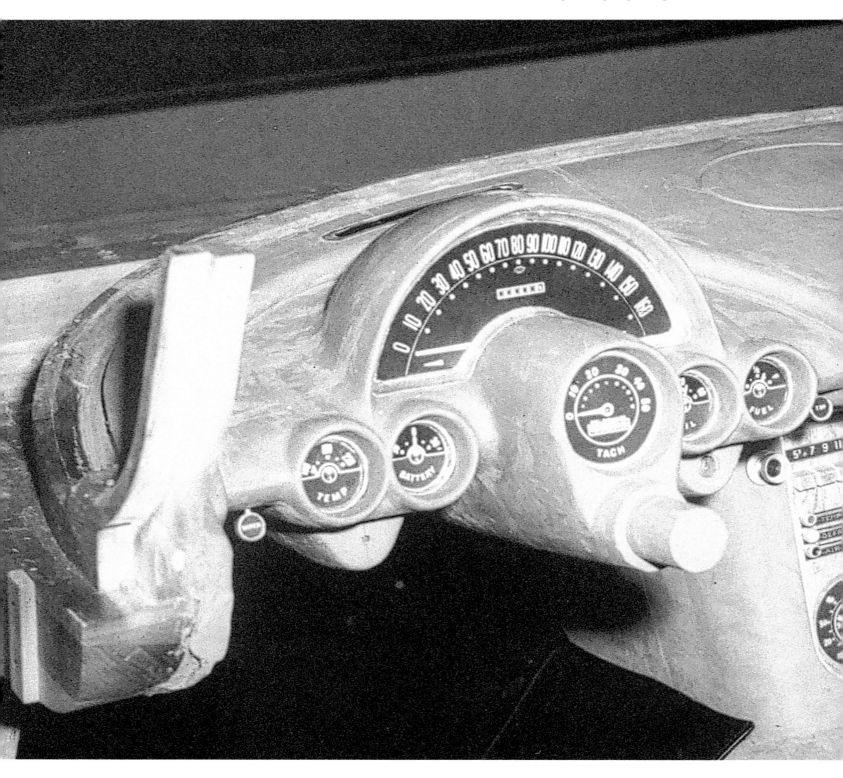

Below: Even in carbureted form, by 1959, the 283 cu. in. V-8 could produce around 270 bhp.

Harley Earl's retirement was announced on December 1, 1959. He had been with General Motors for thirty-two years and had, during that time, become the undisputed style arbiter of the American automobile industry and thus, perhaps, the most influential designer of all time. His influence would linger; he had, of course, personally penned designs for the Corvette through 1961. He would be succeeded by his pupil, the

forty-six-year-old William "Bill" Mitchell, who, like all good pupils, couldn't wait to have a crack at the teacher's job. The third-generation Corvette, which Mitchell was to make his own, was still three years away in the metal, but was already taking shape on the drawing board. The shift would be incremental but the end result would be totally radical.

Complex as it is, the detailing of the 1959 comes together extremely well.

This Page:
The 1959 Corvette, like its predecessors, managed to be both Beauty and the Beast at the same time.

Next Page:
Harley Earl retired in December 1959 after over thirty years' service to GM. The fabulous styling of the Corvette of that year is a fitting tribute to a true genius.

Right: A 1959 Corvette is a car to brighten the dullest day.

Next Page: And perfect for fun in the sun!

1961 saw the first real evidence of a new hand on the tiller. The reworking was subtle but the direction that the styling was being taken in was becoming ever more apparent. The tail section gave the clearest clues: The deck was flattened, losing its voluptuous curves and becoming sharper-edged—a distinct break with the "feel" created by the first major restyle in 1956. Bill Mitchell had already created the XP-700 show car and the racing Sting Ray and the 1961 car showed the influence of both. Chrome was gently removed, the gleaming "teeth" of the radiator grille being replaced by a more subtle mesh. Underneath, the radiator was now crafted in aluminum. Interior refinements included dual sun visors, a warning light for the parking brake, and windshield washers. It's interesting to note that nearly 90 percent of customers opted for manual transmission, and of those, two thirds wanted the four-speed, now with an aluminum housing. A fully optioned 'Vette could now run a standing quarter in 14.2 seconds, hitting 99 mph; 60 mph could come up in 5.5 seconds and the top speed was close to 130 mph.

Left: The "ducktail" rear of the 1961–1962 restyle incorporated recessed quad lights that have become a Corvette trademark.

Styling revisions for 1961 were mainly about simplification. A mesh grille replaced the chrome teeth—silencing one of the last echoes of the 1953 car.

Left: The Corvette has always been a fine example of good breeding, retaining its unique character from generation to generation.

Next Page: Note the opening trunk lid, soon to disappear, and the instruments, now neatly grouped in front of the driver.

The 1962 Corvette is regarded as a classic among classics and is a true "watershed" car. It was the last to have benefited directly from the hand of Harley Earl. It was the last to utilize Bob McLean's cross-braced chassis design that dated from the 1953 original and was still going strong and coping with more than double the horsepower of the truck-engined, bus-tired original. The small-block V-8, originally displacing 283 cu. in., was bored out an eighth of an inch to 4 inches and had its stroke increased by a quarter of an inch to 3.25 inches, raising the capacity to 327 cu. in. Maximum output, with fuel injection, was now 360 bhp. The Corvette could now hit 100 mph in a quarter of a mile from a standing start, covering the distance in 15 seconds, even without fuel injection! Styling was sharpened up and toned down. Contrast-color coves were deleted—an abandonment of what was, perhaps, one of the earliest and most effective examples of "retro-styling," echoing the glamour of the 1930s—in favor of a cleaner and more unified look that was to typify 1960s style. As ever, the Corvette was showing the way. Ed Cole gave way to Semon E. "Bunkie" Knudsen as general manager and Corvette production rose to 14,531. Base price was $4,038, rising to around $5,500 for a fully loaded example. That meant that the buyer could have the performance of a Ferrari for under half the price and without the rust problems. Thanks to the combined efforts of Mister Earl, Mister McLean, Mister Cole, Mister Curtice, Mister Keating, Mister Barr, Mister Duntov, and Mister Mitchell, and others, the 1962 Corvette was, effectively, unimprovable.

SPECIFICATIONS

1962
Wheelbase 102"
Length 14' 9"
Width 5' 11"
Weight 3,137 lb.
Transmission 2-speed auto,
3-speed manual, or
4-speed manual
Brakes 11" drum
Engines
Base 327 V-8
Compression 10.5
Gross Horsepower 250

Option 583 327 V-8
Compression 10.5
Gross Horsepower 300

Option 396 327 V-8
Compression 11.25
Gross Horsepower 340

Option 582 327 V-8
fuel injection
Compression 11.25
Gross Horsepower 360

Above: A detachable hardtop had been available since 1956, instead of the soft top or additional to it at extra cost.

Below & Right: Only the 1962 had the fluted cove and rocker panel trim.

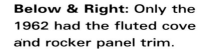

Above: The 1962 Corvette has become a classic among classics—unlike the ill-fated Corvair in the background.

Right: Even though a completely new model was imminent, 1962 sales shot to 14,531.

The 1962 still looks cool after over forty years. Thanks to its rustproof bodywork and bulletproof engineering, a surprising number of them are still around to be admired.

Right & Next Page: The shape of things to come. The rear view of the 1962 is very close to that of its successor, the Sting Ray. The trunk lid is the main giveaway!

As ever, the Corvette was equally at home on the road and the track. Here we see a 1962 parked quietly in the driveway, while Dick Thompson takes his to the SCCAA Prod championship.

1963–1967
Sting Ray! Sting Ray!

Below: The Sting Ray was one of the first cars in the world to benefit from wind-tunnel testing to improve aerodynamics. Full-scale mock-ups like this one were employed so that adjustments could be made prior to production.

When something can't be made any better, the only thing to do is make something better. Bunkie Knudsen was a second-generation General Motors man. His dad, William Knudsen, had been made head of operations at Chevrolet back in 1922, when K. W. Zimmerschied moved to the post of assistant to the president of the company, then Pierre du Pont. William was known as "Hurry Up" Knudsen in recognition of his enthusiasm for production. It was during Knudsen's reign, in 1927, that Chevrolet's valve-in-head, "Stovebolt" six-cylinder engine, which would, of course, eventually power the first Corvette, went into production. On the tenth anniversary of that model's introduction, a totally new car was to be offered to the public. By now, the Corvette was perceived as a

Above: The styling of the Sting Ray drew heavily on Bill Mitchell's Mako Shark styling exercise—seen here with a Plexiglas hardtop—of 1961.

separate entity from run-of-the-mill Chevrolets and so to distinguish the all-new model from its predecessors it was given an additional title: Sting Ray. Much has been made of the likelihood of the name having been derived from Bill Mitchell's fondness for fishing trips, and the styling does have certain undeniably piscatorial elements. Mitchell had shown his beautiful Mako Shark concept car in 1961, anticipating many of the features that would appear on later production Sting Rays. It seems most likely, however, that the inspiration for the Sting Ray racer's styling came not from a fish but from a cat. Jaguar had wowed the world with their beautiful E-Type (XKE) in 1961, but the car had first appeared as a racing prototype in 1956. The production E-Type was a road-going development of the C-Type and D-Type racers, which had performed spectacularly at Le Mans and elsewhere. The D-Type, along with its even more glamorous stablemate, the XKSS, provided much of the inspiration for the Corvette SS Racer, which received a favorable review from Juan Manuel Fangio, probably the greatest race-car driver of all time, after he tried it out at Sebring in 1957. The SS inspired the Sting Ray race car, which in turn inspired the XP-720. The XP-720 became the 1963 Sting Ray. It is worth noting, in support of this argument, that Mitchell himself drove an E-Type Jaguar.

Above: The SS Racer underwent as many revisions as the road models, serving as a rolling test bed and, in the process, reaching 183 mph.

Like the Jaguar, the new Corvette was offered in both convertible and coupe form. The look of the car also echoed Larry Shinoda's Q car essays, but it was from the XP-720 that Duntov developed the Sting Ray's ladder-frame chassis and suspension layout. Taking the XP-720 chassis, with its five cross-members, as his template, Duntov had the passenger compartment positioned as far back as was feasible and the center of

Above: Family likeness is seen in the tail treatment of the all-new Sting Ray.

gravity lowered from 19 to 16.5 inches. Ground clearance would be a mere five inches. All this, combined with the independent rear suspension that Duntov was adamant about including, would ensure an enviable combination of secure road holding and excellent ride quality. The 102-inch wheelbase of the original roadster—also echoing a Jaguar, the XK120—was cut back to 98 inches. The drivetrain was routed right

Above: Duntov's "Ladder-Frame" chassis allowed the new car to sit lower on the road than the original X-Frame.

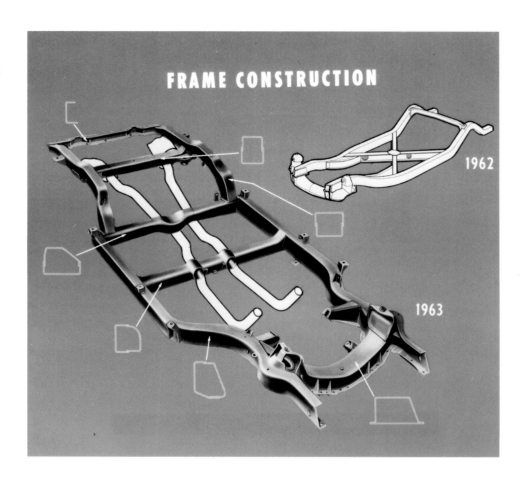

Opposite Top: The Sting Ray was beautifully balanced, to the eye and on the road.

Opposite Below: The Sting Ray's GRP shell was subjected to lengthy stress-testing prior to being put into production.

down the centerline and kept as low as possible. Weight distribution was almost perfect at 51/49 percent.

In order to justify the cost of the rear suspension, which was fiercely resisted by the GM management, Duntov assured the suits that its inclusion would help to push sales toward 30,000. His confidence was justified. In the first year of production, almost 22,000 Sting Rays found homes, the coupe and the convertible being equally favored.

Again like the Jaguar, the Corvette was among the first road cars to benefit from serious attention being paid to its aerodynamics. In the mid-1950s, the D-Type, shaped by Malcolm Sayer, could run to 180 mph with a (comparatively) long-stroke, six-cylinder engine of 3.4 liters (210 cu. in.). Wind tunnel testing had as much as anything to do with determining the Corvette's basic shape. Despite the fact that there was more steel and less GRP in the new car, kerb weight was down a little on the 1962. Oddly, neither version had a trunk lid, so access to the luggage compartment was via the cockpit. It couldn't have been much fun trying to slot a heavy suitcase behind the seats, but there was compensation, perhaps, in the car's ravishing, unbroken lines. The most celebrated detail of the coupe was its "spine." This was a continuous line that ran from

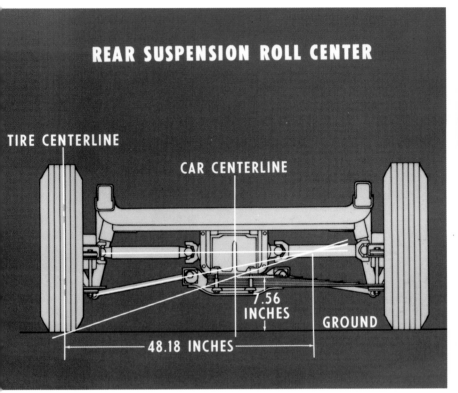

REAR SUSPENSION ROLL CENTER

TIRE CENTERLINE

CAR CENTERLINE

7.56 INCHES

GROUND

48.18 INCHES

CORVETTE FRONT SUSPENSION

Above: Duntov insisted on independent rear suspension for the Sting Ray—and he got his way.

the tip of the tapering bulge in the hood to the center of the deck, bisecting the rear window on the way—like the tail of a real stingray. Nobody liked it at the time, but now it's considered classic. It is, if nothing else, concrete evidence of Mr. Mitchell's corporate clout. The elegant side coves were gone, but a ghostly reminder of them remained in the shape of a pair of dummy vents on each front fender. A neat, lift-off hardtop was supplied for the roadster, and the coupe's doors cut into the roofline to make entry and exit from the low-slung cockpit easier and more decorous—short skirts were fashionable in the 1960s, remember?

The steering still used a recirculating ball system but was a new design that gave tighter response. There were still quad headlights, but they now hid themselves away when not in use. The lights were raised by electric motors when switched on. Brakes were now self-adjusting; an alternator was fitted in place of a generator. The car had an alloy clutch housing and a lightweight flywheel. For the first time, a full leather interior was offered. Competition was back on the agenda and a host of mouthwatering options were offered with this in mind. These included upgraded suspension, including heavy-duty torsion bars, Al-Fin aluminum brake drums, metallic brake linings, and cast alloy wheels with knock-off hubs. A 36.5-gallon fuel tank was also available, which presumably occupied most of the luggage space that was inaccessible anyway.

Fitted with the Turbo Fire 327, a 1963 Corvette could achieve speeds in excess of 150 mph. Competition options could improve both speed and handling dramatically. The checkered flag badge now seemed wholly appropriate.

Specifications

1963

Wheelbase 98"
Length 14' 8"
Width 5' 10"
Weight 3,035 lb.
Transmission 2-speed auto, 3-speed manual, or 4-speed manual
Brakes 11" drum
Engines

Base 327 V-8
Compression 10.5
Gross Horsepower 250

Option L75 327 V-8
Compression 10.5
Gross Horsepower 300

Option L76 327 V-8
Compression 11.25
Gross Horsepower 340

Option L84 327 V-8 fuel injection
Compression 11.25
Gross Horsepower 360

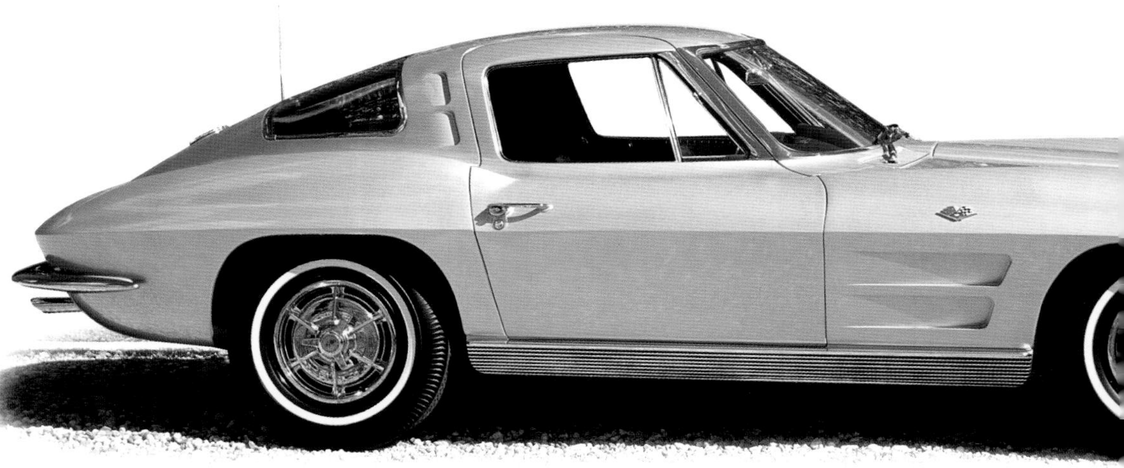

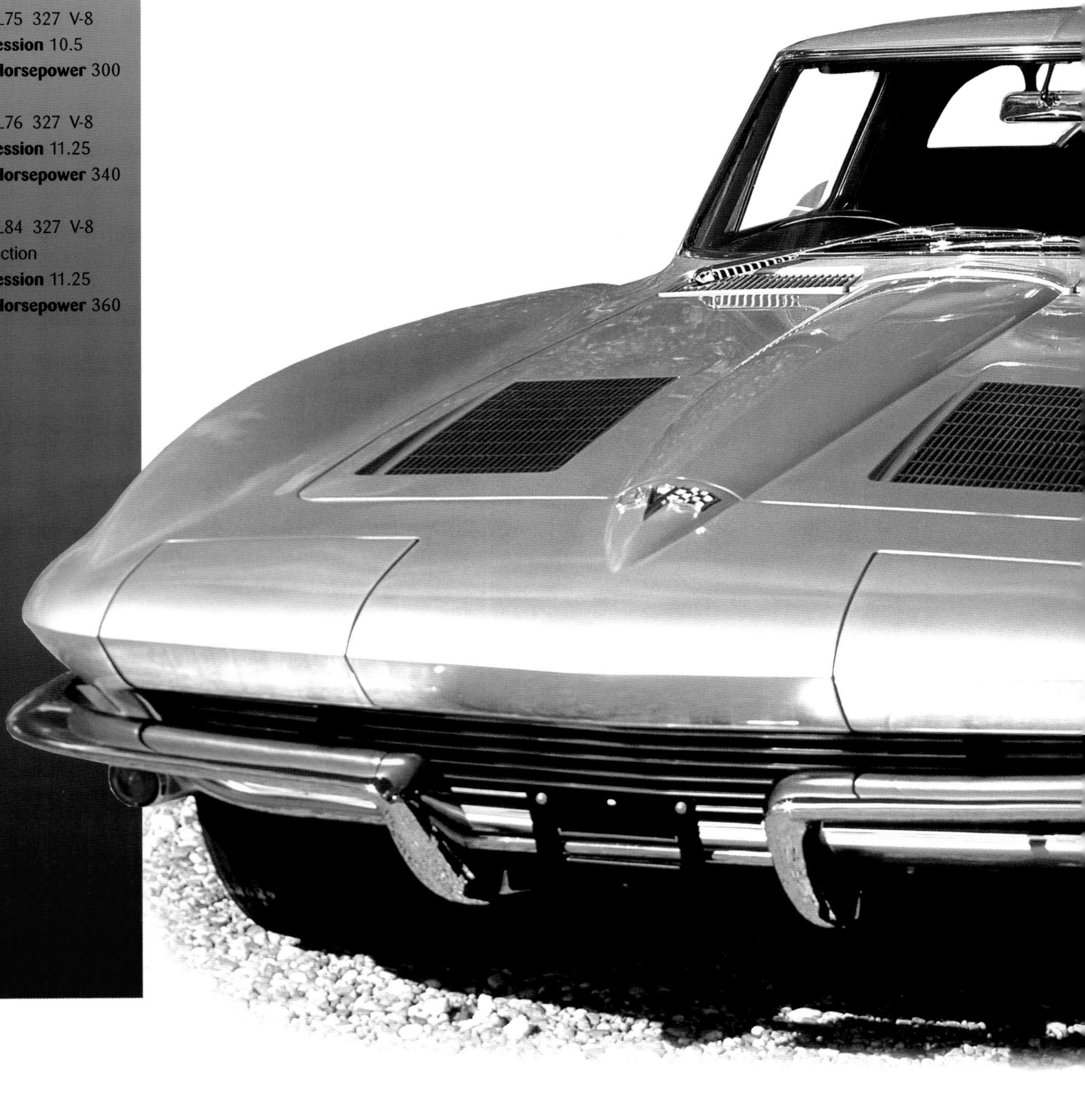

Below Top: For 1963 only, conical gauge centers were bright satin finish.

Below Bottom: The headlight pods were swiveled by electric motors.

Above: A full-size, painted mock-up of the Sting Ray is rolled out into the daylight for appraisal.

Opposite Top: The beautiful proportions of Mitchell's design are shown clearly in this overhead view.

Opposite: Genuine knock-off hubs were an optional extra.

The 1963 Sting Ray was the fastest and best-handling Corvette to date. Fitted with a 3.70:1 rear axle, a 1963 Corvette tested by *Sports Car Graphic* recorded a 0–60 mph time of 5.6 seconds and a standing quarter-mile time of 14.1 seconds with a terminal speed of 102 mph. Top speed was measured at 151 mph. Forty years later, that's still impressive. Carroll Shelby was instrumental in having a number of Corvettes bodied in aluminum by Scaglietti in Italy, in an attempt to produce a lightweight, racing derivative. He ended up putting a Ford motor into a space frame chassis from AC Motors of Thames Ditton, thus producing the legendary Cobra, which, though it often bettered the Sting Ray on the track, could never hope to catch it in the marketplace. The 1963 Sting Ray was the only truly "original" Corvette between the 1953 original and the fourth-

Left: The deletion of the center spine from the rear window gives the car a more open feel and improves rear visibility.

Next Page: His 'n' hers 1964s.

American sports cars all look alike.
'65 CORVETTE

Corvette is America's one true sports car—has been for years.

But Corvette is also two body styles. Five engines and three transmissions available. Plus enough other equipment you can order to make any kind of sports car you want.

For aficionados, there's the snarly Corvette. Ordered with a 375-hp Ramjet fuel-injected V8, 4-speed fully synchronized shift, Positraction, cast aluminum wheels, special goldwall tires, genuine wood-rimmed steering wheel, telescopic steering column,

special front and rear suspension and special exhaust system.

For boulevardiers, there's the plush Corvette. Ordered with a 300-hp V8, Powerglide, power brakes, steering and windows, tinted glass, genuine leather seat trim, AM/FM radio, and air conditioning.

And if you're a bit of both aficionado and boulevardier, you can get all kinds of in-between Corvettes, part snarly and part plush.

Every Corvette gives you 4-wheel disc brakes, fully independent suspen-

sion, retractable headlights, and a sumptuous bucket-seated interior as standard. At a very reasonable price compared to any car near its class.

Now you know why America has only one sports car; with all those different Corvette versions, who needs any more?

Corvette Sting Ray

Chevrolet Division of General Motors, Detroit, Michigan

Above & Right: A big-block V-8 was available for 1965, starting out at 396 cu. in. and producing up to 425 bhp.

Left: Chevrolet's advertising underlines the point that there is only one, true, American sports car.

The 1965 Corvette, full on and in detail. Note how the doors cut into the roofline to allow easier access, but the luggage compartment has no access at all!

Although the Sting Ray was gaining ever more power and sophistication mechanically, the exterior styling became even simpler and more serene.

All-round disc brakes were now offered at a very reasonable $64.50. Lap seat belts were provided, but apparently not always worn.

Previous page: The 1965 Sting Ray's front fender vents recalled the gills of the Mako Shark and would become a Corvette hallmark.

Above: Both interior and exterior detailing was distinctive but remarkably restrained for the period.

Left: The fitting of the big-block V-8 had necessitated the creation of a very genuine, ventilated "power bulge" in the hood.

1966
There's no substitute for cubes

This phrase has long been regarded, by mostly envious Europeans, as an example of American lack of refinement, but it is, in fact, merely a paraphrase of a remark made by one W. O. Bentley, "If you want more power, build a bigger engine." Nobody ever accused Bentley of vulgarity, did they? Whatever, in 1966 the Corvette went the whole nine yards. Duntov introduced the Mark IV engine, restored to its full 427 cu. in. capacity. In order to avoid problems with insurers, Chevrolet deliberately underquoted the Corvette's maximum power output, leaving it, without explanation, unchanged at a mere 425 bhp. The true figure was probably around 450.

Depending on the axle ratios, a "big-block" Corvette could accelerate to 60 mph in under 4.8 seconds and still have a top speed of 140 mph. With higher gearing, upwards of 160 mph was easily achievable.

The 427 Corvette was half a ton heavier than the Shelby Cobra, with around the same horsepower, so it was less than a threat to the Ford-powered AC in the SCCA A-Production class—as if the Cobra was ever a "production" car—but the 'Vette could still win laurels in endurance racing. Penske's team ran twelfth overall in the GT class at the 1966 Daytona Continental.

Previous Page: The Mako Shark II remains one of the most striking automobile designs of all time and would provide the inspiration for an entire generation of Corvettes.

Left: Styling was progressively simplified through 1966 and 1967, revealing how beautiful the lines of the Sting Ray were.

Next Page: The side-mounted exhaust was an optional extra that seems superfluous today.

A new model was slated for 1967 but the body shape had caused problems in the wind tunnel and so Duntov decided to postpone its introduction for a year. This meant that 1967 was the final year for the Sting Ray but it turned out to be its greatest. On the track, Penske's team placed first at Sebring. On the road, the Corvette was taken back to its most beautiful basics, stylewise, by the total elimination of extraneous decoration, though a massive air-scoop was necessary on the hoods of cars fitted with the 427 V-8. A reversing light was a unique feature on the 1967 Corvette, as was the centrally mounted hand brake. A sign of the times was the fact that the hardtop was available with a black vinyl covering. The real highlight, however, was the production of around twenty L-88s. The L-88 chassis was equipped with the F-41 suspension package plus massive brakes and the Positraction differential. This version of the 427, running on high-octane fuel, could produce a mind-boggling 560 bhp.

Previous Pages: Fuel injection on the small block was deleted in 1966; the carbureted 427 was cheaper and more powerful.

Left: By 1967, the last year of its life, the Sting Ray's styling had been pared back to the point where it resembled a designer's outline.

The 427 cu. in. V-8 approached 450 bhp, giving a 1967 Sting Ray so equipped better performance than many contemporary exotics. Acceleration was incredible, with 60 mph coming up in under five seconds.

Once again, as in 1962, a Corvette design would be abandoned at the peak of perfection. It's hard to see how the 1967 could have been further improved. Note the reversing light— what else was there to add? A trunk lid, maybe?

Sting Ray sales had peaked in 1965 at 26,171 and even in 1967, when the model was supposed to have been replaced, they were still over 23,000. In total, 120,000 Sting Rays had been sold, of which 72,500 were roadsters. The Sting Ray was the shortest production run of any Corvette design but has become one of the most sought after. It gave Americans some of the most exciting motoring in history and banished the myth of the U.S. being unable to produce a "real" sports car. The 1967 Corvette was quicker and faster than the Ferrari Testarossa of 1992.

The third-generation Corvette took its inspiration from the Mako Shark II show car of 1965, which was in turn derived from the XP-775 experimental of 1961—so that the model that followed the Sting Ray, in some ways predated it.

Left: The big-block V-8 seems to be weighing this 1967 model down somewhat.

Next Page: Without power bulges or side exhausts, the line of the small-block 1967 Sting Ray is pure perfection.

Right: Development problems dogged the Sting Ray's successor, delaying its release by a year and thus allowing this exquisite automobile to enjoy an "Indian summer" in 1967.

Below: 1967 sales approached 23,000, despite a new model being imminient. General Motors had produced a particularly great automobile.

1968–1982
The Mako Generation

Below: Having waited over a year to try out the striking new Corvette, unfortunately some reviewers concluded that it was unfit to test.

Shark infested waters

According to automotive legend, Bill Mitchell caught a shark on one of his fishing trips. This was reputedly on the island of Bimini, in the Bahamas, sometime in 1961. His XP-775 experimental, Corvette-based styling exercise of 1961, conducted in association with Larry Shinoda, is obviously predator-inspired. With its gill-like vents, pointed nose, gray-fade paint job, and all-around menacing aspect, it was christened the Mako Shark; all it needed to complete the illusion was fins—but this was

the 1960s already! The production car that followed almost immediately, however, was called the Corvette Sting Ray and the ridge that ran from its nose to its tail was definitely more ray than shark. The car also took styling clues from another manufacturer, as had already been discussed. Mitchell's macho/mako musings continued through the single-seat XP-15 to the Mako Shark II of 1965.

The Mako Shark II caused a sensation at the 1965 New York International Auto Show. Whereas the original Mako Shark had drawn on existing Corvette styling details, the Mako Shark II was a totally new concept, with a flowing fender line and a pinched waist, giving it the now familiar and classic "soda bottle" shape. Concealed lights were retained and complimented by concealed windshield wipers that eventually found their way onto production cars, briefly. The Mako Shark II had digital instrumentation and a rear window with electrically operated louvers that somehow added to the subaquatic effect. With its sinister, ground-hugging profile, the car drew huge crowds and much admiring comment when it was shown in the style capitals of Europe, including London, Paris, and Turin.

Below: The Mako II's lines are still there, but aerodynamics had caused big problems.

Unfortunately, the styling of the Mako Shark II was matched neither by its handling characteristics nor by its driver-friendliness. The transition from show car to production model was overseen by David Holls of the Chevrolet studio. Utilizing the Duntov chassis from the 1963 Sting Ray,

Above: From some angles, the 1968 Corvette is distinctly reminiscent of certain Ferrari models.

the new body showed an alarming tendency to lift under acceleration. This was cured, or at least addressed, by cutting vents in the front fenders and by increasing the spring rates. Due to the wasp-waisted body design, the passenger compartment was narrow and cramped and the low roof line inevitably restricted headroom. To add to the new model's birth pangs, Duntov had been hospitalized in New York and thus the development work was given over to the Chevrolet sedan team. Just as Bunkie Knudsen had boosted production by introducing a second work shift on the Corvette line, so his successor, Pete Estes, eager to emulate Knudsen's achievement, immediately initiated a third. This time, however, increased output would be demanded of an unfamiliar design, with unfortunate consequences.

Top Left: The interior was cramped due to to the "wasp-waisted" body styling.

Top Right: Vents in the front fenders were practical rather than decorative, as they helped to correct a nasty tendency for the nose to lift.

The impressive styling of the third generation of Corvettes was not quite matched by the build quality—at least on early examples.

Launch of the new Corvette was delayed a year. Despite the public's evident desire for a new model, 1967 Corvette sales had dipped rather than dropped dramatically, from 27,720 to 22,940. The excitement caused by the Mako Shark II, coupled with the postponement of the new Corvette's release, could confidently be believed to have increased the eager anticipation of potential customers. Sadly, even after the design had

Top: A good proportion of Corvette drivers opted for the four-on-the-floor manual transmission option.

Bottom: Engine options included the mighty L88, which was capable of producing 560 bhp. Even the "base" 350 cu. in. V-8 now pushed out a respectable 300 bhp.

Above: A T-bar had to be inserted in the roof of the coupe to counter chronic body shake.

received an additional year's revision, the 1968 Corvette was still seriously underdeveloped when offered to the public. The car was greeted by the motoring press with reactions that ranged from apathy to hostility. It looked new and yet there was no new chassis and no new engines; *Road & Track* pointed out that the styling, which had seemed so radical in Mako Shark II form, now seemed derivative, resembling the Ferraris of some years earlier. The car was bigger and yet there was less room in it; it had been necessary to tilt the seats back, the angle increasing from twenty-five degrees to thirty-three degrees, to allow for the low roof line. This resulted not only in discomfort for both driver and passenger but also meant that they were continually sliding forward. The ride was harsh, the cockpit was noisy, and there was no luggage space. The Targa roof was replaced by a T-Top, which incorporated a central brace in an attempt to reduce body shake. The car's overall appearance was striking and yet the finish and detailing were poor, the concealed windshield wipers worked intermittently at best, the body panels fitted very badly, and the paint finish was amateurish. The hardtop leaked, the engine was difficult to start and had a tendency to overheat . . . *Car & Driver* returned theirs, saying that it was unfit to road test.

SPECIFICATIONS

1968

Wheelbase 98"
Length 14' 11"
Width 5' 10"
Weight 3,220 lb.
Transmission 3-speed auto,
   3-speed manual,
   or 4-speed manual
Brakes 11.75 disc
Engines
   Base 327 V-8
   Compression 10.5
   Gross Horsepower 300

   Option L79 327 V-8
   Compression 11.0
   Gross Horsepower 350

   Option L36 427 V-8
   Compression 10.25
   Gross Horsepower 390

   Option L68 427 V-8
   Compression 10.25
   Gross Horsepower 400

   Option L71 427 V-8
   Compression 11.0
   Gross Horsepower 435

   Option L89 427 V-8
   Compression 11.0
   Gross Horsepower 435

   Option L88 427 V-8
   Compression 12.5
   Gross Horsepower 430
      (probably true 550)

Below: The shape of the new 1968 was a sensation. Bystanders would ask new owners, "Where are the wipers?"

Right: The Targa roof coupe was a new feature for 1968, became a Corvette tradition, and started the trend away from convertibles.

Below: The chromed rack was a popular option, always fitted by the dealer, not the factory. Backup lamps were hidden beneath the rear bumpers.

Left: Base engine was this 300 hp 327. The vacuum canister at the left of the picture lifts the wiper flap.

Opposite Inset: The 'Vette's bloodline was clearly visible in much of the third generation's detailing.

Top Inset: Despite the availability of incredible engines like the L88 and the ZL1, the small-block remained the most popular choice, giving up to 350 bhp output.

Left: The new Corvette was seven inches longer, but it had less room for passsengers and luggage.

Back to the future

Zora Arkus-Duntov had risen from his sickbed to discover that his unofficial title of Corvette's head of design was no longer acknowledged and that he was now answerable to the very team that had failed so lamentably to develop the 1968 into the refined and desirable production model that it ought to have been. Happily, at exactly this time, one John DeLorean, who was later to achieve worldwide notoriety due to another severely underdeveloped sports car, became general manager at Chevrolet, replacing Pete Estes. DeLorean, to his eternal credit, immediately appointed Duntov to the official position of chief engineer of Corvette.

On the plus side, the Corvette was now fitted, exclusively, with all-round disc brakes and the buying public seemed unfazed by the poor publicity; the first year's sales total rose to 28,566. It was obvious, however, that further refinement and a lot more attention to quality control would be necessary if these sales were to be sustained.

Left: Mr. Duntov may be smiling, but his third-generation Corvette of 1968 had received some vicious criticism.

More is less

The new Corvette was lower than its predecessor but it was also longer, wider, and heavier. Overall length had increased from 175 in. to 182 in. and most of this was due to the greatly increased overhang at the front— the wheelbase remained unaltered from the Sting Ray's 98 in. Track increased at both front and rear, up from 56.5 in. to 58.7 in. and from 57.0 in. to 59.4 in., respectively. Weight increase was an overall 150 lb. so that the car weighed in at around 3,400 lb. Chassis revisions were minor. The rear springs were stiffened to help reduce nose lift under acceleration, and on big-block optioned cars the front coil rates were also increased. The rear roll center was lowered, which, coupled with the suspension tuning, further encouraged understeer, an acknowledged Corvette trait. Combined with the fitting of wider (7 in.) wheels, however, all this served to increase the car's cornering limit from 0.75 g to 0.84 g. By 1969, critical comments were becoming marginally more positive. The stiffening of the springs and fitting of wider wheels had improved handling markedly, and the old Powerglide automatic transmission had been replaced by the greatly superior Turbo Hydramatic. Overall finish was infinitely better, but the car now had a harsher ride and the cockpit was still cramped. Even after a revision of the interior that had cost $120,000 and produced an increase in shoulder room of a half inch each side, the Corvette was still, as *Car Life* put it, "One heck of a big car for two people and almost no luggage." A trunk rack was supplied to increase the car's carrying capacity, but utilizing this reduced rear vision to zero— leaving aside the fact that what was effectively an outside trunk was hardly in keeping with a futuristic automobile. In 1969, the Stingray name was revived—this time as one word instead of two. In spite of all its shortcomings, its noisiness, its harsh ride, and its general brutishness, the Corvette was still a very powerful, fast, and sexy car.

For 1969, the standard wheel width was again increased, from 7 in. to 8 in. The small-block engine had its stroke increased, raising capacity to 350 cu. in., and was offered in two states of tune, delivering 300 bhp and 350 bhp (one horsepower per cubic inch), respectively. Four versions of the 427 were available. With triple, two-barrel Holley carburetors, a four-speed, Muncie manual gearbox, and a 3.55:1 rear axle ratio, a 435 bhp version could accelerate from rest to 60 mph inside six seconds and a standing quarter mile was possible in fourteen seconds. Crude as the ride quality still was, *Car Life* magazine's comment was no less than the truth: "You'd better believe that it takes a lot of car to catch this bear!"

Bear? Either way, there was even a ZL1 option, with an all-aluminum block and dry-sump lubrication, developed by McLaren for CanAm racing, that weighed 100 lb. less than the mighty L88 option and produced something in the region of 560 bhp. Admittedly, this option increased the price of a "standard" Corvette by some 60 percent, up from around $5,000 to $8,000, and only two road-going examples ever left the factory, but it was available for anyone with deep pockets and strong nerves.

Even the small-block Corvettes drew favorable comment now. Only a year after they had considered the new model too tacky to test, *Car & Driver* decided that the car now offered an interesting problem for the prospective purchaser to ponder. "The small-engine Corvettes are marginally fast and extraordinarily civilized. The large-engine Corvettes are extraordinarily fast and marginally comfortable." You paid your money and you made your choice. The third shift had raised output to 38,762—an increase of ten thousand from 1968. On November 7, 1969, the 250,000th Corvette came off the line and it looked like the problems were over. In fact, they were just about to begin.

Above: Sales continued to climb,
despite the carping of some,
increasing by 10,000 in 1969.

Previous Page: The critics criticized but the buyers bought—these two obviously thought it was great! Sales in 1968 were up to nearly 29,000.

Inset: Even with the roof sections removed, the cockpit was still a tight fit for many drivers.

Next Page: In 1969 the Stingray name was revived—but this time as one word.

With up to 400+ bhp available,
a 1969 Corvette with a Muncie
box could run to 60 mph in six
seconds and cover a quarter mile
in fourteen seconds.

The 1970s

In 1970, an auto workers' union dispute hit production at the St. Louis factory. Whatever the general grievances of the labor force, things couldn't have been helped by the increased pressure they were under due to the introduction of the third shift. The net result was a two-month delay in the

Below: By 1970 the fender vents had received a mesh-effect revision that matched the dummy radiator intakes in the nose.

1970 model reaching dealers' showrooms. This, in turn, led to a massive drop in orders and production slumped to 17,316—the lowest for nearly a decade. The 1970 Corvette was—and is—therefore a rare car, but unlike a lot of "limited-production" machines, it was—and is—definitely desirable. Despite their troubles, Chevrolet had continued to revise, refine, and

SPECIFICATIONS

1970

Wheelbase 98"
Length 14' 11"
Width 5' 10"
Weight 3,285 lb.
Transmission 3-speed auto
or 4-speed manual
Brakes 11.75 disc
Engines
   Base 350 V-8
   Compression 10.25
   Gross Horsepower 300

   Option L46 350 V-8
   Compression 11.0
   Gross Horsepower 350

   Option LT1 350 V-8
   Compression 11.0
   Gross Horsepower 370

   Option LS5 454 V-8
   Compression 10.25
   Gross Horsepower 390

There were many improvements for 1970, including:

Opposite Top Left: Improved seats.

Opposite Top Right: New cast fender grille.

Above: Rectangular exhaust outlets.

Styling changes were minimal and incremental. The four "gills" that cut into the front fenders were replaced by a grille, and this was echoed in the (false) radiator intakes up front. It had been noted that the lower sections of the body were susceptible to damage from stones thrown up by the wheels. This was addressed by flaring the wheel arches. The twin tailpipes were changed from round to rectangular. The seats were improved, giving better support and more headroom, and improved access to the luggage area—for there was still no trunk lid. Inertia-reel seat belts were fitted as standard.

Left: 1971 was the last year that horsepower was quoted as a gross figure. The figure for a 1971 base 350 engine (270 bhp) would, the following year, be shown for the 454.

Right: The price of fresh air: 1971 was the year that compression ratios had to be drastically lowered to allow Corvette engines to run on lead-free fuel and thus reduce harmful emissions.

Getting the lead out

In 1971, GM's president, Ed Cole, decreed that all of the corporation's automobiles were to be made to run on 91-octane fuel. This was in response to the approaching Clean Air Bill that would ban the use of lead as an additive in gasoline. Up to this point, engines like the Corvette's big-block, 427 cu. in. V-8 had been intended to run on 103-octane "premium" fuel that contained a high level of tetraethyl lead as an antiknock ingredient ("knocking" being preignition). The only way that this reduction in octane levels could be accommodated was via the drastic lowering of compression ratios—down to levels not seen since the very first Corvette rolled off the line at Flint in 1953. This meant that the small-block V-8 now had to run with a compression ratio of 8.5:1, producing a modest 270 bhp at 4,800 rpm. The LT1 version was cut to 9.0:1, producing 330 bhp at 5,600 rpm. The big-blocks suffered similarly: the LS5's output fell to 365 bhp at 4,800 rpm and the LS6's to 425 bhp at 5,600 rpm. The 1971 Corvettes were still hardly underpowered. The LS6 was capable of reaching 60 mph from a standing start in five and a half seconds, and a standing quarter took it around fourteen seconds, reaching 105 mph. Top speed was in excess of 150 mph. Even though some muscle cars of the period were now claiming much higher outputs, few, if any, of them could match the Corvette's speed and acceleration—or its handling—on the road.

The versatile T-Top coupe now outsold the convertible Corvette by a ratio of five to three. The fallout from Ralph Nader's infamous 1965 treatise, *Unsafe at Any Speed*, about poor auto design in general—and the inherent, lethal flaws of Chevrolet's 1960 Corvair Monza in particular—was filtering down to automakers in the form of ever more draconian directives. The effect of Nader's writings were profound and affected all automobile makers, including those overseas. Any foreign manufacturer wanting to import cars into the United States would have to ensure that they conformed fully to the relevant federal and state legislation. The effect of *Unsafe at Any Speed* was global. Initially, there was massive resistance to Nader's pronouncements, which were seen by some as an assault on personal liberty and by others as a restraint of trade. This resistance eventually broke out into open hostility in the form of "dirty tricks." In March of 1966, James Roche, then president of General Motors, made a public apology to Ralph Nader, admitting that

Opposite and Next Page: An autoworkers strike had cut production in half in 1970. Sales of the 1971 'Vette crept back up to over 21,000.

Next Page Inset: Attention had been paid to the aerodynamic problems of the Mako II, especially the tendency of its nose to lift under acceleration.

the corporation had paid people to spy on Nader in an attempt to obtain evidence with which to discredit him.

It seems hard to believe that an attempt to point out the inherent danger of certain automobile designs could have resulted in such behavior, or, indeed, that such designs could have been allowed to proceed to production. The conflict between corporate profit and personal integrity is still with us, but, hopefully, new technologies will ensure that potentially lethal design flaws never get beyond the drawing board or at least the computer display. By the beginning of the 1970s, the days of the all-American convertible were already numbered. There were no styling changes made to the Corvette for 1971, but the new ZR1 package was offered. This was another pure competition option, comprising of the LT1 small-block engine mated to a heavy-duty, four-speed transmission. The ZR1 also had an aluminum radiator and carefully revised suspension with stabilizer bars and heavy-duty springs and shock absorbers. Power brakes were fitted as standard but power windows were not an option, along with power steering, air-conditioning, rear-window defroster—or even a radio. A total of only eight ZR1s were produced.

Previous Page:
Despite their trials and
tribulations, the Corvettes
of the early 1970s remain
extremely desirable
automobiles.

Right: Comfort was now
being emphasized alongside
performance. The 1971
Corvette could still be called
a "sports car" but it could
hardly be called "spartan."

Performance continued to be deemphasized. From 1971, horsepower ratings were quoted as SAE (Society of Automotive Engineers) net, a standard that measured "true" output in the sense that it allowed for such mundane, everyday items as air cleaners, pumps, and mufflers. Thus LT1's output was now shown as being down from 350 bhp gross to 255 bhp net. In 1972, the LS6 option was deleted, leaving the 365 bhp LS5 as the most powerful 'Vette available. The car's desirability was undiminished, however, and, as if to prove this, the previously optional antitheft alarm system was now fitted as standard equipment. In an effort to reduce production costs, and so keep showroom prices competitive, Chevrolet was gradually reducing its options lists—in both the cosmetic and the performance departments—for all their vehicles.

Left: Performance-sapping legislation in the 1970s caused more emphasis to be put on "luxury" features.

Next Page: 1972 saw Corvette performance begin to fall below par.

Left: The 1973 still had exposed back bumpers and optional exposed luggage-carrying facilites.

Left Inset: The taillights were still round but the tailpipes were now rectangular.

Middle & Right Inset: Bright, fiberoptic exterior light monitors had been deleted from the center console. Maximum power was now 275 bhp (net) from the one remaining 454.

Top: Automatic transmission remained a popular option and seemed appropriate to the gentler, "touring" image that the Corvette was trying to assume.

Right: Radial tires were now standard equipment, but their speed rating was lower than the old bias-belted ones.

The 454 big-block V-8 had only one more year to run and its output would fall by 5 bhp in 1974, but loyal devotees still bought Corvettes and 1973 sales production was well over 30,000.

It is interesting to compare the Mako Shark II with the 1973 Stingray on the next page and the 1974 that follows. From the advent of the "soft" tail, the shape of the car would gradually shift away from its forebear's form and toward that of the coming generation.

Previous Page: Magnificent as it is, the 454 cu. in. V-8 was a brave choice during the oil embargo of 1974.

Right: The color-coded, impact-absorbing front and rear sections blend perfectly into the 1974 Corvette's lines—a stark contrast to the grotesque battering rams fitted to many cars at the time.

Previous Page: 1976 was the last year of the Stingray name. Even without a roadster in the lineup, Corvette sales were up to 46,550.

Right: Sadly, America's bicentennial year was the first year that a Corvette roadster was not offered since production had begun in 1953.

Next Page: Without a full convertible top, the wide-open spaces just weren't the same anymore.

The Corvette had become an institution. It remained unchanged, effectively redundant, and yet had an army of loyal supporters. Despite the fact that the design was becoming increasingly irrelevant, getting heavier and slower and more expensive as every year rolled by, the Corvette had become a legend in its own, long lifetime. To demonstrate this, in 1976 the

base price broke $10,000 for the first time: the L48 version of the small-block produced 180 bhp; the L82 210 bhp; there was no convertible roadster offered; sales increased to 46,558. The following year, with no improvements having been made to the car and the Stingray name abandoned, sales improved again, to a record 49,213.

Beware the ides of March

March 15, 1977, saw the 500,000th Corvette come off the line in St. Louis, but there would seem to have been little cause for celebration among either the producers or the purchasers. Blind brand loyalty might be sufficient to keep a small manufacturer like England's Morgan Motor Company going, with order books full for a decade in advance, but it could hardly be expected to sustain sales figures of 50,000 units a year. Nevertheless, as the same old Corvettes came off the line, the styling basically unchanged from 1968 and the performance considerably lower than it had been in 1968, there were customers waiting for them. 1978 was the silver anniversary of the model; it was twenty-five years since the original Polo White Corvette was produced, with its Stovebolt Six motor and its two-speed transmission and ill-fitting side screens. To mark this occasion, the coupe's styling was finally revised. The upright rear window, set between tapering pillars, was replaced with full, wraparound glass. Glass roof panels were also available as optional equipment; the car's interior became, instantly, much lighter and brighter than before. All the cars produced in 1978 were specially badged and there was a special anniversary edition as well, with a two-tone silver paint job and exclusive aluminum wheels. The engine options remained exactly as before: the 350 cu. in. small-block in either 185 bhp or 220 bhp. Two, four-speed manual gearboxes were available, plus a three-speed Turbo Hydramatic.

Previous Page: The 1977 Corvette was no longer branded as a Stingray, but production nevertheless rose inexorably toward 50,000.

Left: 1978 was the Corvette's twenty-fifth anniversary and all cars got a new, wraparound rear window.

Right: This 1978 special anniversary coupe is "unspoiled." The optional, bolt-on spoilers from the pace car replica were incorporated into the front and rear sections for 1980.

Inset: The stylish special edition wheels were made of cast aluminum alloy.

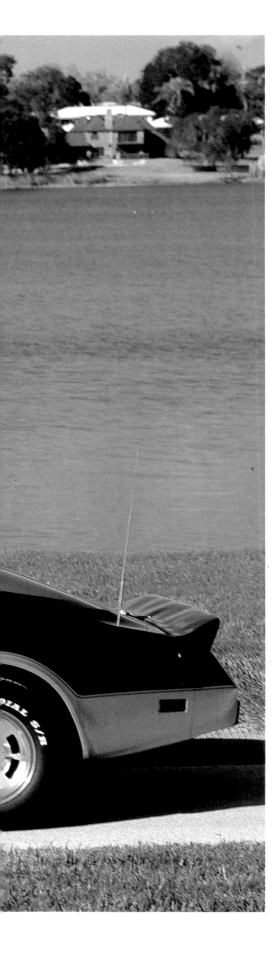

Still setting the pace, sort of

The other special edition for 1978 was the pace car replica. The Corvette had been selected as the official pace car at the Indianapolis 500 that year and Chevrolet capitalized on this by producing a cosmetic copy. The replica featured bolt-on spoilers front and rear, plus a two-tone, black and silver paint job and silver-gray interior trim with lightweight, leather-trimmed bucket seats. A set of decals, identical to those used on the actual Indy pace car, were supplied, to be applied to the car should the purchaser so desire. Considering the fact that, in the case of both the anniversary edition and the pace car replica, the differences from the standard model were entirely cosmetic, the premium on these models was considerable: $3,653 on top of the base price of $10,000. Sales fell, but only slightly, to 47,887. Some collectors were so eager to get their hands on a pace car replica that they bid up to as much as $6,000 over the already inflated list price.

Left & Next Page: The 1978 Indianapolis 500 official pace car replica came with authentic decals, which the owner could choose to have applied to the bodywork or keep as a souvenir.

SPECIFICATIONS

SPECIFICATIONS

1978

Wheelbase 98"

Length 15' 6"

Width 5' 10"

Weight 3,550 lb.

Transmission 3-speed auto or 4-speed manual

Brakes 11.75 disc

Engines

Base L48 350 V-8

Compression 8.5

Net Horsepower 185

Option L82 350 V-8

Compression 9.0

Net Horsepower 220

The unique pace car wheels had a red stripe and no black paint on their center caps.

The pace car replica's two-tone, black and silver paint job was both striking and attractive. The interior was in silver.

The silver paintwork of the anniversary model could be combined with a choice of interior colors. Note the electric window lifts and mirror adjustment. By 1982, automatic transmission would be fitted as standard.

All 1978s had special silver anniversary badges.

SPECIFICATIONS

1978

Wheelbase 98"
Length 15' 6"
Width 5' 10"
Weight 3,550 lb.
Transmission 3-speed auto
   or 4-speed manual
Brakes 11.75 disc
Engines
  Base L48 350 V-8
  Compression 8.5
  Net Horsepower 185

  Option L82 350 V-8
  Compression 9.0
  Net Horsepower 220

Above: All 1978 Corvettes had this twenty-fifth anniversary emblem.

Left: The optional L82 engine had dual cold air snorkels and ribbed aluminum valve covers.

The silver anniversary Corvette looks more like a luxury tourer than a sports car. This was very much a sign of the times, which, as we know, change.

Previous Page: About the only change for 1979 was that all cars now came with the improved, lightweight seats from the pace car replica.

Right: 1979 saw sales soar above 50,000 for the first time in the Corvette's history.

Right: Despite all the complaints that had greeted the new Corvette in 1968, sales in 1979 topped 50,000.

The following year the pace car replica's spoilers became an option on all cars and its specially designed, lightweight, bucket seats came as standard. In 1980, the spoilers were incorporated into the deformable front and rear body sections, the marginal improvement in drag coefficient helping to keep down fuel consumption. In a further bid to squeeze more miles per gallon out of the car, attention was paid to weight reduction. The Corvette had been piling on the pounds for over a decade: up from around 3,000 lb. in 1968 to pushing 3,500. In order to reduce this excess avoirdupois, the GRP panels were (literally) slimmed down, as was the glass. Steel, in the front chassis cross-members, differential housing, and exhaust manifold, was replaced by aluminum. Kerb weight came down to under 3,200 lb. The other big reduction was on the dash panel. The 1980 speedo only read to 85 mph, presumably on the assumption that nobody would ever dream of exceeding the newly imposed 55 mph mandatory speed limit by more than thirty miles an hour—even in a Corvette.

Left: By 1980 Corvette engineers were making changes, invisible to the naked eye, to reduce weight and increase performance.

Next Page: Turbocharging was in vogue in the early 1980s and attempts were made to develop a Turbo Corvette.

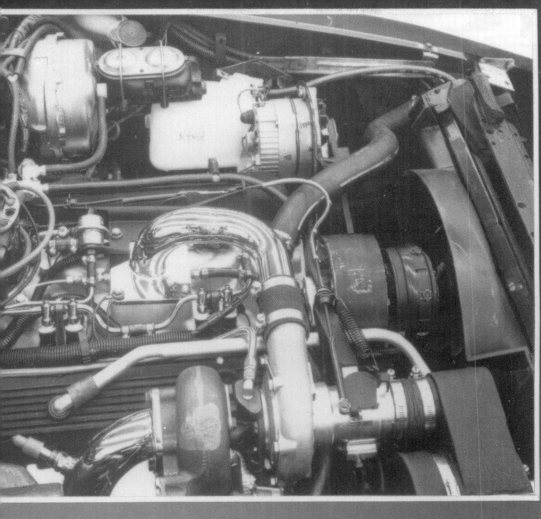

Although forced induction could provide a bag of additional power, it was heavy on fuel and didn't complement the silky-smooth power transmission that the Corvette's V-8 still delivered.

Next Page: The nose and tail of the 1980 Corvette were neatly reworked to improve aerodynamic efficiency.

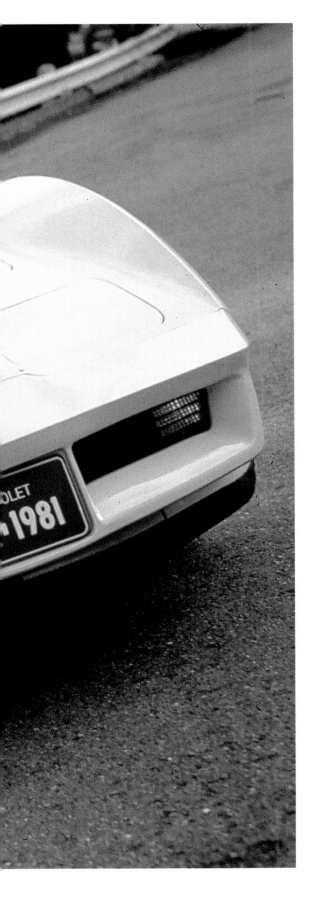

Attention to meaningful detail continued, however. In 1981 the rear leaf spring was made in fiberglass, saving twenty-five pounds. The one remaining 350 power plant, the L81, now featured magnesium rocker covers, a stainless-steel exhaust manifold, and GM's Computer Command Control engine management system. Output was unchanged but inflation pushed the base price above $15,000—but at least that included a six-way power driver's seat.

The biggest shift to occur with the beginning of the new decade was the transfer of Corvette production from St. Louis to a brand-new, state-of-the-art, dedicated Corvette facility at Bowling Green, Kentucky. The move to Kentucky showed that not only was the Corvette continuing, but that a new model was in the offing. Production had peaked at 53,807 in 1979, but then dropped sharply to 40,614 in 1980. The new 55 mph speed restriction couldn't have helped.

Left: Corvette sales had peaked in 1979 at 53,807. By 1981 they were down to just over 40,606. It seemed almost like the 'Vette was going out of fashion.

Next Page: Integrated spoilers and weight reduction helped to keep fuel consumption as low as possible.

Right & Next Page: The 1981 model was fitted with the L81 350 small-block, which incorporated such features as magnesium rocker covers, a stainless-steel exhaust manifold, and a computer-controlled engine management system.

Left: 1982 was the last of the Mako-generation Corvettes. After fifteen years, the resemblance to the original was still discernible—but just barely.

In the nick of time

The 1982 Corvette was intended to be the last of the Mako Shark generation, and another "special edition" was produced to mark the model's fifteen-year run. Once again, the outward appearance was unchanged but for a paint job and some new alloy wheels. This time the public wasn't impressed—even by a long-overdue, lift-up rear window that allowed exterior access to the luggage area—especially when they saw the sticker price of $22,537, for less car than they could have had back in 1968 for $4,663. Sales collapsed to 25,407, the lowest for a decade. The country was in recession and there was a new energy crisis.

What hardly anybody had noticed was that, once again, elements of a completely new design were being trailed ahead of time. For the first time since 1965, the 'Vette was a "Fuelie": the 350 small-block was fitted with a computer-controlled, twin throttle body "Cross-Fire Injection" system. For the first time since 1955, the 'Vette came with automatic transmission as standard, with no manual option; the new Turbo Hydramatic system was a four-speed, with fuel-efficient lock-up on the torque converter for all gears except first.

The Corvette was about to reinvent itself again, but first, an intermission...

Right: The opening rear window was an immensely welcome, long-overdue innovation. The dropping of the manual transmission option wasn't quite so exciting.

Top: Fuel injection was now back after a lapse of some sixteen years.

Above: A special collector's edition interior trim package in tones of silver and gold marked the end of the Mako Shark era.

Right: With its special silver paint scheme, the collector's edition sold 6,759 copies.

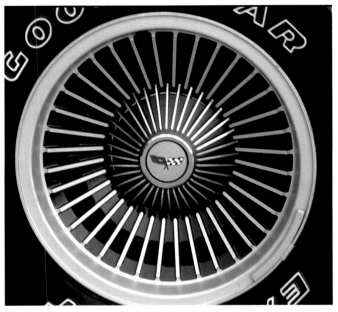

Top: The collector's edition also had special wheels.

Above: Cross-fire injection sounded very impressive, but by 1982 the cumulative effect of successive government legislation had been to emasculate the power of the engine.

Left: From this angle, the lines of the Mako Shark II can still be made out. The model had lasted, through troubled times, some fifteen years. In 1982, just over 25,000 examples were produced.

1983

The 1983 Corvette is the rarest automobile on earth. It is more exclusive than the Alfa Romeo 2900B Lungo, more elusive than the Gordon-Keeble, the Facel-Vega, or the Isotta-Fraschini, and more evasive than the Maybach. The 1983 Corvette makes the Gaylord look like a straight eight, because . . . there was no 1983. To the Corvette enthusiast, 1983 does not exist. It's like when the calendar was changed from the Julian to the Gregorian system in 1582, and the day after October 4 was October 15. How annoying would that have been if you had tickets for the big game on October 9? If that had happened in 1983, India wouldn't have taken control of the Punjab, the Chinese Communist Party people would have been spared its worst purge since the Cultural Revolution, Lech Walesa wouldn't have received the Nobel Peace Prize, the Baltimore Orioles wouldn't have won the World Series, and there would have been no thirtieth anniversary collector's edition Corvette—and there isn't.

Left: A British-registered, 1978 silver anniversary edition. It seems unlikely that the owner will find himself parked next to another one very often.

1984–1996
To Play the King

Below: The 1984 Corvette's chassis and body were entirely new and radically improved.

George Orwell was wrong: 1984 ushered in a brave new world!

During the fifteen years of the Mako generation's reign, another generation had quietly assumed control of the Corvette family business. Zora Arkus-Duntov, who had done so much toward transforming the Corvette from a sports car into a supercar, had retired almost a decade earlier, his place being taken by Dave McLellan. Bill Mitchell put away his pencil in 1977, to be replaced at the drawing board by Jerry Palmer,

head of the Chevrolet Three Studio. Palmer and McLellan were to form a close partnership, merging form and function fully for the first time. Their departments, working in parallel, would produce a completely new, perfectly integrated package that took into account all of the disparate demands created by the desire for safety, handling, performance, comfort, and charisma. Their combined talents produced a car that— like a good coffee or a good scotch—blended smoothness, strength, sophistication, and style while retaining its own unique identity. Along with GM's director of design, Chuck Jordan, and vice president of design staff, Irv Rybicki, Palmer and McLellan managed to produce a completely new car that was still, unmistakably, a Corvette. The trail that they followed to reach this happy conclusion, however, traversed a vast area of ground that had been explored previously—and mapped in detail—by the above-mentioned pioneers.

Below: The family likeness is still visible—the fender vents hark back to the 1950s—but the 1984 model provided an entirely new platform for development.

Top: Even the badge had been revised for 1984.

Bottom: The sixth-generation Corvette had, once again, benefited from extensive aerodynamic research, resulting in a beautifully smooth profile.

Exploring the alternatives

The new car's clear, genetic heritage—its "family likeness"—would have been far more difficult to maintain had Chevrolet decided to follow Ford down the mid-engine path. By the late 1960s, Ford's mid-engined GT40 had established itself as one of the all-time great sports/racing cars, winning at Le Mans for four straight years from 1966 to 1969. Reacting to this, Frank Winchell, then head of research and development at Chevrolet, produced an experimental, mid-engined prototype called the XP-880. This car was shown at the New York Auto Show in 1968 (the same year that the Ford GT40 took the Sports Car Championship) as the Astro II and generated considerable interest. It was at precisely this time, as mentioned earlier, that Zora Arkus-Duntov had returned from the hospital to discover that his position of authority in the Corvette hierarchy had been severely undermined during his absence. Duntov immediately sought to reassert his dominance and produced his own mid-engine design, the 1969 XP-882, which carried the small-block V-8 mounted transversely behind the passenger compartment, driving the Turbo Hydramatic transmission via chains with the driveshaft passing through the oil pan—an idea later utilized in the Lamborghini Countach. A couple of prototype chassis were produced and the idea of a mid-engined Corvette began to gather momentum. John DeLorean, taking over as Chevrolet's new general manager, however, soon silenced such discussions by pointing out that such a design would be hugely complex and unfeasibly expensive to develop for volume production.

Heedless of the supposed practical problems, both Duntov and Bill Mitchell had really warmed to the idea of a mid-engined car. Meanwhile, over in Italy, Alejandro De Tomaso, an ex–cattle baron turned race car driver, whose anti-Peron opinions had forced him to leave his native Argentina, was busily mounting Mustang V-8s, centrally, in sinuous bodywork designed by Giorgetto Giugiaro.

The resultant hybrid was named the Mangusta; *Mangusta* means "mongoose," and mongooses kill cobras. The combination of Italian styling and American muscle produced a heady cocktail of looks, performance, and, crucially, reliability. British Motor Car Distributors in California ordered 200 Mangustas and it became an instant style icon.

British Motor Car Distributors was owned by Kjell Qvale, who subsequently acquired Jensen Motors of England and imported the Interceptor III, another magnificent example of successful, trans-Atlantic crossbreeding. In association with Donald Healey, Qvale also produced a small sports car called, naturally enough, the Jensen-Healey. As a young man, Healey had collaborated with George Mason to produce the Nash Healey, one of the very first trans-Atlantics. The Jensen-Healey was fitted with a Lotus-developed engine. Although, as we all know, the mid-engined Corvette idea was never brought to fruition, certain parts of this complex story became intrinsic elements in the development of the latest generation of cars.

Anyhow, Ford bought a controlling interest in De Tomaso, along with their subsidiaries: the Ghia styling studio, where Giugiaro had worked, and that of Vignale. The next model produced was the Pantera, which featured a Ford 351-C, 310 bhp V-8, mid-mounted in a unitary body, styled by Tom Tjaarda, Ghia's American designer, and engineered by Gianpaolo Dallara, who had created Lamborghini's stunning Muira. When this fabulous beast began to appear in Lincoln-Mercury showrooms, along with predictions of 10,000 a year being produced, Chevrolet's XP-882 was hastily dusted off. This time around, Bill Mitchell was charged with the task of styling a version around a four-rotor Wankel engine. With the Ford/De Tomaso marriage in mind, DeLorean hired Pininfarina to style a two-rotor version as well. Both versions were shown to the public in 1973, to be shelved immediately due to the oil crisis. Even then, and with the departure of Mitchell and Duntov, the idea just wouldn't go away. A prototype named the Aerovette, with a mid-mounted Wankel engine, was produced in 1977. Even though its name conjured up visions of Eastern European airlines, the Aerovette was a striking design and it was widely believed that the 1980s would herald the arrival of an all-new, mid-engined supercar.

In the final analysis, the question of whether the driver ought to sit in front of the engine or behind was settled by . . . the driver. Whereas Europeans are apparently happy to put up with temperamental machinery on the grounds that chronic unreliability is somehow a sign of sophistication, the American motorist is primarily interested in having a

car that will start in the morning without having to have the oil warmed in a pan, and which doesn't need retuning every week. The Corvette sells throughout the United States, from Alaska's cold to the Everglades. It's a performance car but it must perform at all times and in all places, regardless of heat, cold, rain, snow, or relative humidity. American drivers like to be able to get in and out of a car without having to take a course in yoga and to able to hear the stereo, or even the passenger, above the induction roar. The Corvette works. It's worked since 1953. If it works, don't fix it.

So . . . 1984 saw the release of a new Corvette that was reassuringly the same and excitingly different. The styling, compared to previous incarnations, especially its immediate predecessor, was remarkably restrained. Signature features— the foldaway headlights and the four, big, round, recessed taillights—were there, as were the wraparound rear window from the later Makos and the front fender vents that harked right back to the indented coves of the 1956 reworking. The line was now much smoother and less aggressive but still purposeful and muscular.

Left: The difference between the 1982 and 1984 Corvette is subtle. The newer car is on the left.

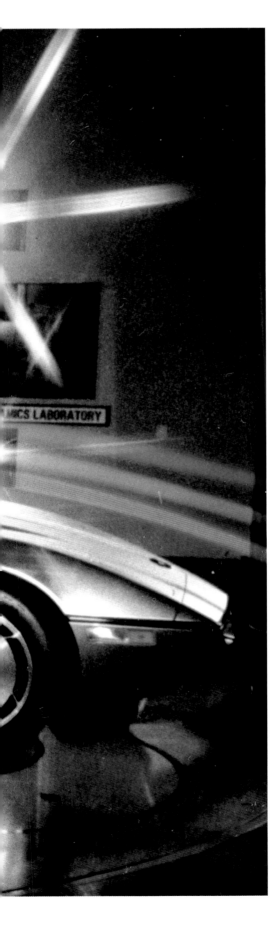

Less is more

The car was smaller on the outside—nearly 2 in. shorter in the wheelbase (down from 98 in. to 96.2 in.)—and almost 9 in. overall, but due to the abandonment of the Mako's "wasp waist" it was bigger on the inside, with 6.5 in. more shoulder room. It was also just over 1 in. lower. Once again, extensive wind tunnel testing had helped produce a shape that was not only easy on the eye but also effective through the air, with a drag coefficient of 0.34. This was a 23.7 percent improvement over the previous body. That meant that, whereas the 1979 Corvette required 143 bhp to propel it at 130 mph on level ground in still air, the Palmer body needed a mere 74 bhp. The T-Roof was superseded by a return to a full "Targa" style design, with a one-piece, removable center panel.

A "rubbing strip" ran right around the car's belt line, serving a triple function: it was decorative; it gave some protection to the paintwork against other people's doors being opened against it, or its doors being opened against other people's paintwork; and it concealed the join between the upper and lower body sections. The whole front section of the body hinged forward for engine access—a vast improvement on earlier models—and what it revealed when opened was as impressive as the coachwork. The engine block and fan casing were painted black, the air cleaner was in die-cast magnesium alloy, the battery was custom-produced in black and silver, the HT leads were custom colored—even the dipstick handles were specially designed. Much of the detail design for the new car was the work of a junior member of the Studio Three team, John Cafaro. The styling of the Corvette now extended to the wiring; it was an exercise in attention to detail not seen since the days of the Cadillac V16s.

Above: The remarkably efficient aerodynamics of the new body shape can be clearly seen in this wind tunnel shot. Drag was reduced by an incredible 23.7 percent, making the car more fuel efficient before the motor was even started.

4 + 3 = 22.5

The motor was the "Cross-Fire Injection" computer-controlled version of the 350 cu. in. small-block V-8 that had been fitted to the 1982 Makos, delivering 205 bhp at 4,300 rpm. Final drive was via either a wide-ratio Turbo Hydramatic, featuring a lock-up on the torque converter in the top three gears, as seen on earlier models or, alternatively, a complex "4 + 3" manual developed from the Borg-Warner T-10 unit.

Opposite Left: The L83 version of the evergreen 350 cu. in. small-block V-8 featured "Cross-Fire" dual-throttle body injection.

Opposite Right: Both wheels and tires were "handed" due to the brake cooling fins of the former and the unidirectional tread patterns of the latter.

Opposite Below: Access to both the engine compartment and the luggage compartment was a radical improvement on earlier models.

The idea of the "4 + 3" system was to evade the "gas-guzzler" tax loading imposed by the Environmental Protection Agency on cars that failed to return an average of 22.5 miles per gallon under simulated "average" driving conditions. Designed by Doug Nash Engineering of Franklin, Tennessee, the system incorporated a secondary set of planetary gears fixed to the rear of the standard transmission to provide overdrive ratios on second, third, and fourth gears. British Triumph TR and Austin Healey sports cars, the Volvo P1800, and others had used a similar, manually operated system, manufactured by the impressively-named Laycock de Normanville, mainly during the 1960s. Doug Nash's computer-controlled system could be overridden by hard acceleration or switched off altogether, but when in use it—not the driver—would determine when to engage the overdrive ratios according to throttle opening, road speed, and gear selection. This drove through a standard final-drive ratio of 3.07:1, with a 3.33:1 offered as an option. The Doug Nash system may have pleased the EPA but a lot of customers remained unimpressed and ordered the optional four-speed, automatic box instead.

The backbone of the design

The most innovative and advanced element of the new design was Dave McLellan's chassis design, which benefited from the experimental, mid-engined cars and mirrored the thinking of Englishman Colin Chapman in the small, but perfectly formed, Lotus Elan, which also had fiberglass bodywork. Duntov's ladder frame, which had served the Corvette admirably since the first Sting Ray in 1963, was now replaced with a single, aluminum C-section beam that ran through the center of the car connecting the front and rear axles. Over this was placed a one-piece, robot-welded "uniframe" to which the fiberglass body panels were bonded. This chassis, together with the extensive use of weight-saving materials in areas that included the front and rear suspension control arms, the A/C compressor, the brake master cylinder, the mounts for the power steering and the alternator, the transmission casing, the driveshaft, and the radiator fan, reduced the kerb weight of the new car from 3,232 lb. to 3,087 lb. The front suspension monoleaf was now fabricated, like the rear's, in glass-reinforced plastic.

The lack of cross-members in the chassis frame enabled Palmer to achieve a lower roof line without any loss of headroom. By passing the exhaust system, with its attendant catalytic converters, along the broad, central tunnel that carried the driveshaft between the massively improved

seats—with optional power adjustment that included lumbar support—
he brought the floor of the passenger compartment down to ground
clearance level. The hood line was also lower, this being achieved by
deleting the carburetor option in favor of fuel injection as standard,
seating the engine fractionally lower, and locating the steering rack
(recirculating balls begone!) forward of it. The new, long-awaited, rack
and pinion steering was power-assisted, with a ratio of 15.5:1 in standard
form and 13:1 in the Z51 competition package, which also included
"gymkhana" suspension that was stiffened to the point that it was too
harsh for normal road use but would permit the car to corner carrying
a lateral force of 0.95 g, the highest ever recorded by an American
production car and higher than a whole lot of European exotics.

Contact with the road was maintained via 15-in. road wheels, 8.5 in.
wide at the front and 9.5 in. at the rear. These were made in cast alloy
and, due to their integral cooling vents for the all-round disc brakes, were
noninterchangeable, either left to right or front to rear. Sixteen-inch

**Below: All 1984s might
have looked like this.
Corvette designers had
explored the potential of
a mid-engined design and
they would continue to
do so, producing amazing
cars like the IMSA GTP.**

wheels became available later in the year and a get-you-home-slowly spare was supplied. P255/50 Goodyear Eagle tires bearing unidirectional "gatorback" tread were produced especially for the car.

Not surprisingly, the new model was extremely well received by both press and public. The Corvette was once again a match for any foreign sports car. The complex and unpredictable Doug Nash 4 + 3 gearbox attracted a fair amount of criticism, as did the futuristic dash panel, featuring digital readouts that could well have been inspired by *Star Wars*. In deep space they might have been effective, but in daylight they became illegible. The only other drawback was a base price of $23,360.

Top speed was measured by *Car & Driver* at 140 mph. Sixty miles an hour came up in 6.7 seconds from a standing start and a quarter mile could be covered, from rest, in 15.2 seconds with a terminal speed of 90 mph. These figures confirmed the fact that the new Corvette was "one of the half-dozen fastest production automobiles in the world." For the first time since 1979, sales exceeded fifty thousand units, totaling 51,547.

1984
Wheelbase 96.2"
Length 14' 9"
Width 6' 2"
Weight 3,192 lb.
Transmission 4-speed auto
or overdrive 4-speed
manual
Brakes 11.5 disc
Engine L83 350 V-8
Compression 9.0
Net Horsepower 205

Below: Electric motors powered the headlight units quickly through 270 degrees of swivel, keeping the lenses clean when hidden.

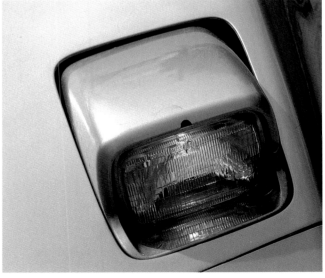

The shape of things to come

The outward aspect of the Corvette was now established and would carry the model through to its fortieth anniversary in 1993 and on to its fiftieth in 2003, allowing for a thousand incremental revisions, refinements, and improvements. As formerly, the development of the car had been leapfrogged: The all-new body concealed the true and trusty 350 cu. in. small-block V-8, with its cast-iron block and its push-rod and

Below: British sports car design influenced the 1984 Corvette, as it had in 1953. Some lucky Brits even got to own one, usually via the dealers at Claremont Corvette of Kent.

rocker-operated valve-gear. This engine was the same one, with the same bore and stroke (4.00 × 3.48 in.), that had graced the line since 1969 and was, even then, merely a stroked version of the 327 that dated from 1962. A new motor seemed long overdue, but the performance limitations imposed by strict emission control laws and fuel economy targets had effectively postponed the pressing need for an all-new power plant for more than a decade. Now, however, the new "backbone" chassis and sophisticated suspension layout were obviously capable of handling a lot more power. The question was how that power would be produced. Federal edicts had by this time become a part of the automotive landscape and a return to the glory days of the 427 was as likely in 1985 as a return to detachable side curtains. It was in 1985, however, that the decision was taken to proceed with a fundamental reworking of the thirty-year-old V-8. That reworking—the ZR1—turned out to be a lot more fundamental than anyone had at first imagined.

It was decided that the revised engine must be capable of returning the same fuel economy as the L98 but would be aimed at the performance levels of Ferrari, Aston Martin, and Porsche. In the words of Chevrolet chief engineer Fred Schaafsma, the ZR1 Corvette was to be "the best-performing production car in the world." The first, somewhat tentative, step along this road was the provision of "Tuned Port" fuel injection, in place of the "Cross-Fire" system, in 1985. This increased output by a respectable, but hardly earth-shattering, 25 bhp. The harsh ride was mollified by a reduction in the spring rates and gas-pressurized shock absorbers were added. An oil cooler was fitted as standard.

Previous Page: The stiffness of the backbone chassis allowed a return to an unbraced open space when the coupe's roof panel was removed.

Above: The digital instrumentation was a cause of much criticism, a greatly exaggerated flaw in a generally excellent design.

Right: The fabulous IMSA GTP cars could reach speeds well in excess of 200 mph with their 1,200 bhp, turbocharged Chevrolet engines. One of their most notorious outings was at Riverside in 1986, when Doc Bundy managed to test one to the limit—and beyond.

Left: Revisions for 1985 included an oil cooler and revised suspension settings with gas-filled shock absorbers.

Above: "Cross-Fire" injection was replaced by the "Tuned Port" setup and increasing compression, releasing an additional 25 bhp. Brakes were now antilock, cylinder heads were aluminum, and response was amazing.

The roadster returns

The big surprise for 1986 was the return of a full convertible Corvette, absent since 1975. A true open-cockpit version of the new body had been anticipated in the basic design and all that was necessary to provide additional stiffness was a chassis cross-member and a lateral beam behind the seats. By happy chance the new convertible was selected as the official pace car for the seventieth Indianapolis 500. The actual pace car was finished in bright yellow, but the replica decals could be supplied with any color, so any 1986 Corvette convertible was a pace car replica.

Overall improvements included the fitting of antilock brakes (ABS) from Bosch. This system was a considerable technological advance, comparable to the introduction of the disc brake. ABS represented a major safety feature, particularly when fitted to a car like the Corvette. For all its good road manners, the car could still deceive an unwary or inexperienced driver with its turn of speed and incredible cornering ability. Power output remained steady at 230 bhp, but that was more than enough for many, bearing in mind the Corvette's lightweight, fiberglass bodywork and aluminum chassis. With the kind of power increases that the designers had in mind, the world's best brakes would become a necessity rather than a luxury. 1986 also saw the introduction of aluminum cylinder heads, a dual exhaust system, and the compression raised from 9.0:1 to 9.5:1.

Left: 1986 heralded the welcome return of a genuine rag-top Corvette, seen here in Pace Car Yellow.

General depression

"Chevrolet has the capability of producing something as good or better than anyone else in the world." This was the confident prediction of ZR1 development manager Doug Robinson at a time when the division, and General Motors as a whole, was going through one of the most traumatic periods in its history. 1986 saw the departure from the GM board of the outspoken, self-made billionaire H. Ross Perot. Perot famously remarked that endeavoring to improve efficiency at General Motors was "like teaching an elephant to tap-dance." This was acid but accurate, for the world's greatest auto manufacturer had been losing its way over the past twenty years, becoming a plodding pursuer rather than the pacesetter that it had been. In short, GM's great leadership had slowly been replaced by mediocre management. Imagination and creativity were frowned upon and decisions deferred increasingly to the bean counters. The result, inevitably, was a succession of automobiles so uninspired and uninspiring that it's a wonder that the shade of Harley Earl never rose up to smite the evildoers. Poor products lead to poor profits as inevitably as night follows day, and GM's income slumped. Perot, with all his innate diplomacy, commented on the management style of then GM president, Roger B. Smith, in a *Newsweek* article: "Since Roger's been chairman they've spent over forty billion dollars in capital improvements, only to lose market share. With the same money, you could have bought Toyota and Nissan and doubled market share. That shows you how big forty billion is." Considering the fact that Mr. Smith had, in all fairness to him, used a considerable chunk of that forty billion to fund the development of computer-controlled production systems, including the wholesale purchase of Electronic Data Systems Inc. (proprietor: H. Ross Perot), this must have been a

Opposite: The swooping lines of the fourth-generation Corvette were perhaps even more effective when the roof was removed.

Left: The 1984 design had been envisaged as an open car from the outset, so stiffening the frame to produce the roadster was straightforward: an X-member below the floorpan, as in 1953!

Above: Detailing was as simple and functional as the overall line of the car. The sum of the parts was one sensational automobile.

bitter pill to swallow. The GM board decided to invest a further three quarters of a billion dollars, wisely, by using it to pay off Mr. Perot in the most dramatic auto industry breakup since Henry Ford II ousted Lee Iacocca in 1978.

GM laid off almost 30,000 workers and a quarter of its white-collar staff. A whole lot of innovative plans and proposals were either cut back or scrapped altogether: Production of the potentially highly competitive Saturn line was reduced by half and plans for GRP bodied versions of the Chevrolet Camaro and Pontiac Firebird were abandoned. The final indignity came when Ford, with only half of GM's automobile sales, showed a greater profit for the first time since 1924.

The 350 cu. in. small-block V-8 was now designated the L98 and produced 230 bhp. Numerous attempts were made to upgrade this engine via forced induction and multivalve heads, but it proved pretty much unimprovable.

Always look on the bright side

In the midst of this doom and gloom, the Corvette team stuck to their principles and followed their own agenda. In their quest for the holy grail of high performance combined with low fuel consumption, some seventeen experimental prototypes came and went. A V-6 engine with massively forced turbo induction could produce a lot of power, but in a manner far too uneven for a driver familiar with the turbine-smooth power delivery of a meaty V-8. Twin turbos were tried on the 350, but the increase in fuel consumption was unacceptable; the Corvette driver had to have his cake and eat it too! As previously described, Wankel rotors and mid-engine layouts had already been weighed in the balance and found wanting. The

search would continue and the searchers would be aided by friends from a distant land, a land where they drive on the wrong side of the road.

At this time Oldsmobile was developing their Quad 4 engine. This was a four-cylinder, with four valves per cylinder, operated by two overhead camshafts, to be offered as an option in their base-range Firenza. Using this design, they eventually managed to extract nearly 200 bhp from

138 cu. in. Olds fans who remembered the old days would have recoiled in horror, no doubt, at this heretical adaptation of the mystical digits 4-4-2, but regardless of that, the Quad 4 showed that the multivalve head was the way ahead, and this, indeed, was the path that the ZR1 design team had decided to follow.

Above: The Corvette's trademark twin taillights remain to this day, having been introduced in 1961.

Left: The new backbone chassis design left a whole lot more room for the occupants than before.

Next Page: By 1986, performance was starting to become more exhilarating; 0 to 60 now took around six seconds. The Corvette was feeling frisky again.

Hands across the sea

1986 had seen the acquisition by GM of a controlling interest in the miniscule British manufacturer of miniscule British sports cars, Lotus. Lotus had built up an enviable reputation in Formula One Grand Prix racing and had also produced some truly great automobiles. The Elan, for instance, featured a fiberglass body mounted onto a backbone chassis. The Jensen-Healey, mentioned earlier, had a Lotus-developed, twin-cam, sixteen-valve engine that was fitted tipped over at an angle to allow for a low hood line. Tony Rudd, Lotus's technical director, had entered into an agreement with GM, about a year before the takeover, to design twin-cam, sixteen-valve cylinder heads for the L98. The main problem for Rudd and his team was that it was a sine qua non that the new engine should be able to fit between the chassis side rails when installed from below on the Bowling Green line. In one of those strange twists of fate, just as it had been the British sports cars of the 1940s and 1950s that had inspired the styling of the original Corvette, so a British sports car manufacturer would supply the inspiration for the engineering of its latest—and undoubtedly greatest—incarnation, fifty years later.

Left: Seventeen-inch wheels with huge Goodyear Eagle tires were available on the 1988 model. After thirty-five years, total Corvette output was close to 900,000.

Left: Access to the engine and its ancillaries was superb, which must have greatly aided those who sought to obtain maximum performance from the L98 for competition purposes.

While the gentlemen of England wrestled with the problem of trying to get more motor into the same space and retaining the existing bonnet line height, the Corvette continued to gain power and refinement back home. 1987 heralded the introduction of roller valve lifters that reduced friction and increased output by ten horsepower to 240 bhp. An optional tire-pressure monitor was offered, which signaled a drop in pressure of one pound per square inch on any wheel, via a dash panel display, to the driver. Also available—at considerable extra cost—was a Twin-Turbo conversion produced by Callaway Engineering. This boosted output to 345 bhp and came as part of a competition package that enabled the car to achieve 175 mph top speed and hit 60 mph from rest in under five seconds.

By this time, having exhausted every avenue of research in their attempts to reinvent the venerable L98, including chain-driven cams mounted at an angle to the cylinder block (tipped into the V to reduce height), Tony Rudd had come back to Dave McLellan with the conclusion that the only way to achieve what was required was to start from scratch. He'd made his point and the decision was made to produce what was to become known as the LT5 engine.

Drivers like Stu Hayner continue to take the Corvette to the track and come home with trophies, as they did back in 1988, for Tom Bell and, more recently, on behalf of Trenton Forging.

Chevrolet dealers Tom Bell of Redlands, California, have been involved with Corvette racing for more years than they probably want to be reminded of. These pictures show that, although fully prepared for the rigors of competition, the car is, underneath, like the ones in Mr. Bell's showroom.

Previous Page: Brakes were beefed up for 1988 and the suspension was modified to prevent rear-end squat under acceleration.

Previous Page Inset: The cockpit display remained pure *Star Wars* and probably appealed to many for that reason.

Right: The 1988 monochrome thirty-fifth anniversary edition trim package was limited to 2,000 copies for sale, plus another 50 for show.

Next Page: The anniversary edition featured white seats and steering wheel plus a tinted glass roof panel. Luxury equipment included air-conditioning, electric seats and mirrors, and a Delco/Bose stereo system. Output was up to 245 bhp.

The thirty-fifth anniversary edition naturally included exclusive badging. Sadly, sales had slipped to under 23,000 cars in total as the base price approached $30,000.

As work on the new engine progressed through 1988, the L98's output rose to 245 bhp, courtesy of a reworked exhaust system and reprofiled cams. The suspension was also revised and larger and thicker brake discs, utilizing dual-piston front calipers, were fitted to redesigned alloy wheels with an optional diameter of seventeen inches. These were shod with immense P275/40ZR Goodyear Eagle tires.

As no cars were officially produced in 1983, the Corvette's thirtieth birthday had passed unmarked. 1988 was the thirty-fifth year of production and a limited edition anniversary model (RPO Z01) was offered. 2,050 coupes were built, finished in white with black detailing and a tinted glass roof panel. The interior was white leather trimmed and equipped with climate control, power seats and door mirrors, heated rear window, and a Bose stereo system. Output for 1988 was 22,789 cars. Total production had reached almost 900,000.

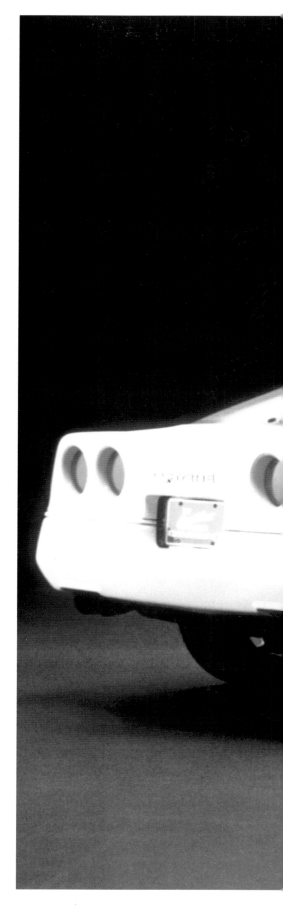

The white bodywork and black roof details of the 1988 anniversary model recalled the original, any-color-so-long-as-it's-white roadster that rolled proudly off the Flint production line in June 1953.

Previous Page: The Corvette Indy was first shown at the Detroit Automobile Show in 1986 and demonstrated how dedicated Chevrolet was to mid-engined Corvette research and image studies.

Right: The Indy featured a monocoque design and was constructed largely from Kevlar and carbon-fiber. The detachable canopy was formed from cast acrylic material. The door opening is similar to that of a Lamborghini Countach.

Right: Fly by wire—the Indy features four-wheel drive and four-wheel steering, both controlled electronically. Its twin-turbo, Ilmore-Chevrolet, Indy Car V-8 was modified to run on standard gasoline.

Right: While Lotus was working on on the LT5 in England, Reeves Callaway, in Old Lyme, Connecticut, was managing to extract over 380 bhp from the pushrod L98 via the use of twin Rotomaster turbochargers. Note the intercooler vents cut into the hood of this 1989 example of his work.

Below: The ZF six-speed was a welcome relief from the complex CAGS 4 + 3 system.

Skip the details

In 1989, tantalizing glimpses of the ZR1 appeared ahead of the rest of it. The first of these took the form of a six-speed, manual gearbox designed jointly by Chevrolet and the highly respected Zahnradfabrik Friedrichshafen AG, (ZF), of Germany. This was a massive improvement on the never-popular Doug Nash 4 + 3, though it incorporated a feature that was to prove controversial, to say the least. As part of the effort to keep fuel consumption out of the "gas-guzzler" league, a system, officially named Computer Aided Gear Selection (CAGS), but also known as the "skip-shift," was employed. On

SPECIFICATIONS

1991 Callaway
Wheelbase 96.2"
Length 14' 10"
Width 6' 2"
Weight 3,440 lb.
Transmission 6-speed manual
Brakes 12" disc
    optional 13" front
Engine twin turbo 350 V-8
Net Horsepower 403
Peak Torque 575 lb. ft.

Above and Right: This 1989 Callaway was returned to Old Lyme in 1993 to have the Callaway Aerobody fitted, and then later modified by them to incorporate special double-ducted intercoolers. It has been timed at 215 mph on a closed track.

Opposite & Below:
Corvettes undergo the
final inspection at Bowling
Green. Every detail—
mechanical, electrical,
interior, and exterior—is
thoroughly scrutinized
before the cars are
dispatched.

light throttle openings (below 35 percent) and at speeds of between twelve and nineteen miles per hour, when the driver moves to change up from bottom gear, the system will lock out second and direct the shift lever across the gate into fourth. This feature, which, in the hands of (and under the right foot of) a dedicated Corvette driver, might never be activated, and combined with a monumentally tall sixth gear for highway cruising, would help to keep the Corvette out of the EPA's bad books. This was despite the fact that it was used in conjunction with the LT5 engine that was just about to turn the Corvette world on its head—or put it back on its feet, depending on how you look at it.

Another whisper on the breeze was RPO FX3 (Selective Ride Control). This was available only on cars fitted with the six-speed gearbox and the Z51 handling package. Developed by GM's Delco division, in association with Bilstein, the SRC system used microprocessors to activate miniature electric motors at the top of each shock absorber. These, in turn, operated rotary valves that controlled the flow of fluid into the piston. The system monitored and adjusted itself ten times per second and functioned during compression as well as during rebound. The driver is offered a choice of settings (Tour, Sport, or Performance) to suit his mood and the driving

Above: Anatomy of a masterpiece: a full cutaway of the legendary ZR1.

conditions. Within each setting the damping rate increases with the car's speed in six, 25-mph steps, from 25 mph to 150 mph. Such is the sophistication of the system, and so much thought has gone into its application, that the speeds at which damping is reduced are set five miles per hour slower to avoid the car constantly shifting between settings while cruising at one of the above speeds. Set to Touring, the suspension will partially absorb ruts and potholes on back roads, while the Performance setting effectively transforms the setup to that of a race car. With the level of performance that SRC was trailing, the ride could never be sufficiently "soft" for limousine comfort, but the system assured that it need be no harder than was absolutely necessary for safety. The base L98-equipped Corvette now retailed at $31,545.

King of the hill

The fourth-generation Corvette had started out as a very good car and had gotten progressively better. The advent of the ZR1, effectively the seventh generation, was to make it into one of the all-time greats. At a cost of somewhere in the region of twenty-five million dollars, Dave McLellan and Tony Rudd achieved the near-impossible in engineering terms. Their goal had been an engine that would produce around 400 bhp and 400 ft. lb. of torque, run smoothly at idle, be docile at low speeds, be capable of (extremely) high speeds and scorching acceleration, but not consume excessive quantities of fuel in the process. The result of their massive investment of time, talent, and money was the LT5.

The engine measures 26.6 x 28.2 x 26.5 inches (11 cubic feet), including its hefty emission control system, allowing it to be fitted into the same space as the L98 unit. Its displacement is exactly the same: 350 cu. in. Output was originally quoted at 375 bhp at 6,200 rpm, torque at 375 ft. lb. at 4,200 rpm. The engine met all U.S. federal emission fuel consumption standards and was able to deliver power smoothly throughout its range, from 650 rpm to 7,200 rpm. The block was cast in aluminum alloy, with "wet" cylinder liners that were hardened with a Nikasil (nickel and silicone) coating. The liners were machined on both inner and outer surfaces to help with heat dissipation. Due to the increased thickness of

the cylinder walls, it was necessary to extend the piston stroke from 3.48 to 3.66 in. in order to keep the overall dimensions within the limits dictated by the space between the chassis side rails.

The resultant, slightly over square bore/stroke ratio placed considerable stresses on the crankshaft, whose design presented one of the trickiest problems for Rudd and his team to solve, and it took them over a year to do so. Chevrolet had initially advocated the employment of an iron crankshaft but in practice this proved to be prone to flex and, under extreme conditions, to failure. Production engines were therefore fitted with nitrified forged steel crankshafts and connecting rods. The crankshaft was

Opposite: Note that the ZR1 is badged LT5, denoting its very special power plant.

Below: Every LT5 motor was individually tested at Mercury Marine before being sent to Bowling Green for installation.

SPECIFICATIONS

1989

Wheelbase 96.2"
Length 14' 9"
Width 6' 2"
Weight 3,225 lb.
Transmission 4-speed auto
  or 6-speed manual
Brakes 12" disc
  optional 13" front
Engine L98 350 V-8
Compression 9.5
Net Horsepower 240

drilled to aid internal lubrication and runs in five oversize main bearings. The crank cradle is formed from a single, aluminum casting that is bolted to the block. The aluminum crankcase is in two sections and the block itself is extensively ribbed and gusseted for maximum strength.

The four camshafts are driven from the crank shaft via a silent, inverted-tooth primary chain between the crank and an idler, which halves the revolutions. A pair of duplex chains with tensioners then transmit drive to the camshaft sprockets. The valves are operated directly by the cam lobes and employ hydraulic bucket tappets to reduce and simplify maintenance. Space limitation dictated a narrow (twenty-two degree) angle between the valves; the camshaft bearings and covers are cast as a single piece.

For the sake of compactness, the starter motor, ignition coils, and A/C compressor are tucked into the V of the cylinder head and other accessories are fitted to cast engine mountings rather than using brackets. The oil pump is driven from the center of the crankshaft, but the water pump, steering pump, A/C compressor, and alternator all share a single drive belt.

Left and Above: Perfect and practical in all its parts, the Corvette ZR1 was one of the most potent pieces of machinery ever to grace a highway.

1988 GRP Corvette bodies process down the Bowling Green line (main picture) to be bonded to their aluminum frames (right). When the engine, transmission, and running gear have been installed, each car is tested on the rolling road (below).

The nature of the beast

The LT5 blocks were produced in Texas, the sump came from Missouri, and the head from England, together with the crankshaft and con-rods. The pistons and cylinder liners were made by a German company, Mahle. Finally, the engines were assembled by Mercury Marine of Stillwater, Oklahoma. Mercury was chosen for its familiarity with lightweight, high-revving speedboat motors.

The bodywork was stock Corvette at the front, but the rear portion was widened to accommodate the massive wheels and tires necessary to transmit the ZR1's prodigious power. The tail was three inches wider than a standard 'Vette and there was nearly six inches more rubber on the road. The rear panel was rounded off more than on the standard car, but the four signature Corvette taillights were squared up! The round, dual tail pipes were replaced by a pair of twin, rectangular tail pipes. It made sense that the main distinguishing features of the ZR1 were put at the back of the car, because that was the part that most other drivers would get to see most often. From the front, probably the only giveaway was the purple-tinted "Koolof" windshield. This was designed to reflect sunlight and thus keep the interior cool, but the fact that it was effectively impervious to infrared made the use of a dashboard-mounted radar detector impossible. This little problem was solved on production models by leaving a small, untinted "window" section at the bottom of the screen—for a remote device to open the garage door, obviously.

Left: The ZR1's "valet key" allowed the owner to convert the character of the car from Lassie to the Hound of the Baskervilles at will.

Right: The rounded tail, which contained squared-off lights, was one of the few clues to the identity of the ZR1, but the rear view was the one that most other drivers got.

Inside, a colorful, if confusing, "aircraft-inspired" digital instrument panel delivered a mass of largely illegible and irrelevant information to a driver who, if he was using his car as nature intended, wouldn't be looking at it anyhow. Similarly, the switchgear was strewn about the cockpit with reckless abandon. None of this would have worried those fortunate enough to be able to purchase one of these fabulous machines, as the driving experience eclipsed all other considerations. A second ignition key, known as the "valet key," enabled the owner to restrict the engine's output to a mere 240 bhp. This was achieved by closing off the larger of the two inlet valves to each cylinder and shutting down one of the injectors. The idea of this device was to limit the exploitation of the engine's full potential to those whom the owner deemed worthy, i.e., to the owner.

When this restriction was removed, a dashboard indicator announced full engine power and the entertainment could truly begin. The ZR1 was capable of sprinting from rest to 60 mph in 4.5 seconds. This phenomenal progress continued, undiminished, until beyond the 130 mph mark, at which point drag would begin to reduce the rate of acceleration. The top speed, which was somewhere in the region of 175 mph, was achieved in

Below Left: The mighty LT5—thirty-two valves, sixteen injectors, 380 bhp, and 375 lb. ft. of torque.

Below Right: Top speed, in fifth gear, was over 175 mph. Sixth gave 42 mph for every 1,000 rpm.

Opposite Left: Familiar flip-up lights.

Opposite Right: Interior fittings and controls recall airplane design. Mr. Earl would surely approve.

fifth gear. Pushing the motor to the rev limit of 7,200, first gear would take the car to 56 mph, while sixth (0.50:1) allowed interstate cruising at 42 mph per 1,000 rpm. Were the engine capable of pulling maximum revs in top gear, the theoretical maximum speed of the Corvette would be 302.4 mph. Maybe it was for this reason that European export models showed 300 on the speedometer. In real terms, the ZR1's performance was equal to that of a Ferrari Testarossa or a Lamborghini Countach, at well under half the price, and with a 60,000-mile warranty. Tuning could raise engine output to 600 bhp, putting a genuine 200 mph top speed within reach for competition use. Chevrolet was hopeful of overseas interest in the ZR1, and details like a one-size-fits-all license plate recess reflected this, as did the ability of the instrumentation to convey information in either imperial or metric units (175 mph is 280 kilometers per hour!), and the use of separate taillight lenses to allow for the fitting of different colors.

1990 was the first full year of production, a small number of ZR1s having been assembled in 1989 for the use of motoring correspondents and road testers. Offered only in coupe form, 3,049 cars were sold, at a base price of $58,995—making the ZR1 the most expensive Corvette of all time by margin of more than $20,000.

By the end of its brief but distinguished career, the ZR1 had gained analog instruments to measure the performance of its upgraded LT5, which finally peaked at 405 bhp. The last batch of 448 cars was delivered in 1995.

Right: The ZR1 is surely destined to become one of the great collectibles in American automobile history—the Duesenberg of the postwar era.

SPECIFICATIONS

1990–1995 ZR1

1990 ZR1
Wheelbase 96.2"
Length 14' 10"
Width 6' 2"
Weight 3,479 lb.
Transmission 6-speed
  manual
Brakes 13" front
  12" rear
Engine LT5 350 V-8
Compression 11.0
Net Horsepower 375
Max Torque 370 lb. ft.

1995 ZR1
Wheelbase 96.2"
Length 14' 10"
Width 6' 2"
Weight 3,512 lb.
Transmission 6-speed
  manual
Brakes 13" front
  12" rear
Engine LT5 350 V-8
Compression 11.0
Net Horsepower 405
Max Torque 385 lb. ft.

Above: 1995 ZR1 with 405 bhp and five-spoke wheels.

Above: The Lotus-designed thirty-two-valve, four-cam engine fitted into the same space as the single-cam pushrod L98. This is a 1989 press car.

Above: Chief engineer for Corvette from 1975–1992, Dave McLellan has arguably had more influence on Corvette history than his predecessor, Duntov. He was the driving force behind the improved 1980–82, the architect of the C4, the father of the ZR1, and the originator of the C5. Since he took over, every Corvette model has been better than the last.

Right: From the outside, the 1990 Corvette coupe was indistinguishable from the ZR1, but was less than half the price.

King for a day

1991 saw a minor restyle across the whole of the Corvette range, with a smoother, slightly more rounded treatment of the front end. Many of the features that had been, initially, restricted to the ZR1 found their way into and onto L98-equipped cars, including the rear panel with its distinctive square taillights. This may have irritated those who had paid a hefty premium for such subtle indicators of exclusivity. Now only the high-level rear brake light and wide tires served to distinguish the king from his loyal subjects. RPO FX3, the "Selective Ride Control" option, was made available on convertibles and so could be had on any car. Such was the excitement that had greeted the announcement of the ZR1 that some people had bid a hundred thousand dollars to secure one but, to their horror, ZR1 sales in 1991 fell back to 2,044—a reduction of a third—and cars were soon being offered at a discount. In fact, total sales fell to 20,729. The ZR1 was now listed as an option package at $31,683—almost doubling the price of the standard coupe. Within two years of its triumphant launch, the ZR1 was being discounted.

Left and Above: 1991 saw the Corvette's lines updated and smoothed out slightly. A "retained power" feature allowed auxiliary systems to function briefly after the ignition had been turned off.

Above: A lot was new in 1992. The Corvette was pushing forty but middle age appeared to recede before it.

Previous Page: The 1991, L98 version of the evergreen small-block 350 produced 245 bhp in its last year as the Corvette's standard power plant.

LT1

David R. McLellan handed over the coveted post of Corvette chief engineer to David Hill in September 1992. In a strange parallel to the ZR1, Hill had worked on Cadillac's Allante—another fine car that failed to persuade the public of its merits. At a time when the U.S. economy in general, and General Motors in particular, was weathering a severe economic storm, it would require courage and determination to steer the Corvette safely through. Despite initial misgivings by some that Dave Hill was not as committed as his predecessor to preserving the Corvette's unique features, he proved more than equal to the task.

The true and trusty small-block V-8 was once again reworked to deliver an additional 55 bhp. Renamed the LT1, it became freer and higher-revving, though with a little less torque than it had produced in its L98 incarnation. Output was now up to 300 bhp and the zero-to-sixty time down to 5.4 seconds, taking what was supposed to be the "cooking" Corvette well into the king's territory. The LT1 received a rapturous welcome from press and public alike, demonstrating once again the innate faith of the American driver in the eternal verities. Four camshafts and thirty-two valves are fine, so long as there's a suitably qualified mechanic within striking distance, but there's something about a cast-iron, pushrod V-8 that inspires confidence in American motorists.

The LT1's compression was up to 10.5:1 even on low-octane gas. This was thanks to the superior cooling abilities of the aluminum cylinder heads, electronic ignition timing that could sense preignition, and reverse-flow cooling. The cooling system was derived from the LT5 engine. Lotus had decided that it would be far more effective to pass the coolant direct from the radiator to the cylinder heads, where it was needed most. This was a reversal of the standard route, which, aided by convection, took the coolant up through the water jackets of the engine block and then allowed it to drop back through the radiator. In order to reverse the flow, a powerful pump was employed, driven directly from the camshaft. The LT1 was the most powerful standard Corvette engine since the heady days of the 1960s, allowing for the difference in measurement standards, and was also employed, in 275 bhp tune, as an option in the Chevrolet Camaro up to 2002. The "Opti-Spark" electronic ignition proved extremely susceptible to moisture early on and modifications, particularly to the venting of the system to prevent condensation, had to be undertaken. Overall, however, the improvements far outweighed the problems and the LT1 was a hit.

Another notable innovation was Anti-Slip Regulation (ASR), a traction-control system developed by Bosch that utilized the ABS sensors on the rear wheels. This detected the onset of wheel spin and simultaneously applied antilock braking to the offending wheel while retarding the ignition and feathering the throttle—it even pushed the pedal back against the driver's foot to let him know that it was operating. In wet and slippery conditions ASR was a valuable safety feature that allowed the car to be driven significantly faster—truly the best of both worlds—although it could cause significant wear increase on the rear brake pads. The system could be disabled for days at the drag strip or the racetrack. With 375 bhp to control, it was especially welcome on the ZR1, but despite this, sales of the Corvette continued to descend: 1992 ZR1 sales were a mere 502, whereas standard hatchback and convertible sales rose slightly, to 14,102 and 5,875 respectively.

On July 2, 1992, the one millionth Corvette was driven off the Bowling Green assembly line. Like the first car to come off the line at Flint, Michigan, it was a white convertible. It would be perhaps the least-traveled Corvette ever produced, as it was destined for the brand new

National Corvette Museum that was being built right across the street—at 350 Corvette Drive. The museum was built entirely with private funds—though Chevrolet was to be extremely generous with their bequests in terms of exhibits—proof of, and memorial to, the affection that the Corvette had earned in the heart of the American public, both drivers and dreamers.

Right: 1993 saw the LT1 small-block producing 300 bhp. The "standard" Corvette could now accelerate to 60 mph in under five and a half seconds.

Forty years on

Sufficient LT5 engines were assembled at Stillwater in 1993 to allow for 448 cars a year to be sold up to the end of 1995, plus a reserve to be held against warranty claims, after which it was discontinued. The arrival of the Dodge Viper RT/10, with its Lamborghini-engineered, all-aluminum, 488 cu. in., 395 bhp, V-10 engine, which had paced the 1991 Indianapolis 500—driven by Carroll Shelby himself—goaded Chevrolet into increasing the output of the ZR1 to 405 bhp. This also served to reestablish the output gap between the LT5 and the LT1. This necessitated a reworking of the heads and the beefing up of the main bearings. Though there was hardly any improvement in acceleration, top speed was boosted to 180 mph.

The LT1 cars got new tires, courtesy of Goodyear again, in the form of directional and asymmetric Eagle GS-C. As previously, these were exclusive to the Corvette for their first year of production. The tread pattern was "handed" as before, but now the tread was designed to allow for the different cornering stresses exerted on the inner and outer edges of the tire. The handling was tremendous, but tire replacement had to be carefully considered, as none was interchangeable with any other. The digital dash was also revised, if not greatly improved. Passive Key Entry (PKE) was introduced, which sensed the proximity of the key fob and unlocked the doors as it approached, or locked them as it receded, tooting the horn to let the carrier of the keys know that all was secure.

The Corvette was now forty years old, but rather than slowing down, it seemed to be just getting into its stride. A metallic, Ruby Red commemorative edition was produced and accounted for about a third of annual sales. The leather interior was color-coded to the paintwork and adorned with various badges and embroideries. Under the hood, the motor was supplied with sound-deadening, polyester rocker covers.

Left: There's little to distinguish this 1994 Corvette from the ZR1 on the outside, except that the King now had five-spoke alloy wheels.

Stylistically, the ZR1 simply disappeared into the "standard" Corvette. Within a year or two, ZR1 performance levels would become standard, too—a standard that very few automobiles approach.

The last of the few

1994 saw the introduction of distinctive—and distinguishing—five-spoke, alloy wheels on the ZR1. With production limited to 448 cars per year—all of which were sold!—these, plus the upgraded, 405 bhp engine, made these cars the most desirable of all, particularly as the option price was reduced to $31,258. The last cars were produced over the following year with the final batch of LT5s from Mercury Marine.

Maybe it was something to do with being over forty—the drivers, not the car—but for 1994 the Corvette's seats were gently widened and their controls relocated to the center console. The newly mandatory, passenger-side airbag was located where the glove locker had been previously, a stowage compartment being incorporated in each of the armrests by way of compensation. The engine's computer management system was rechristened "Powertrain Control Module" (PCM) and extended its influence to the new electronic automatic transmission option. It was now necessary to depress the brake pedal before the selector could be moved out of park.

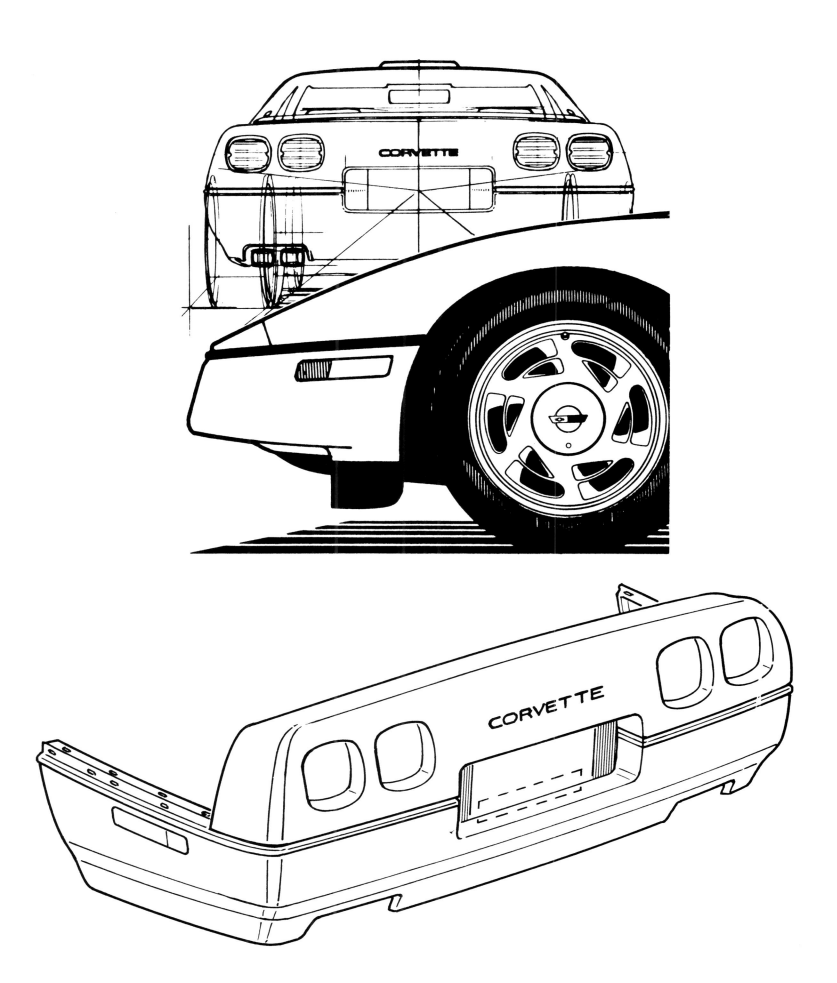

September 1994 saw the official opening of the museum, which attracted some two thousand Corvettes, of all ages, from every state of the U.S. and even from overseas. Chevrolet supplied a number of significant cars, on "permanent loan," for display, including the original Sting Ray and Mako II. Duntov and McLellan both showed up for the festivities and the new management was able to celebrate the fact that sales were up—again—to a total of 23,200. This was in spite of the fact that base prices were now up to record levels; the convertible started at $43,665.

Left: All Corvettes were fitted with the ZR1-style square taillights from 1991.

Right: The 1995 'Vette was so hot, as the English plate on this one seems to imply. It was also so smooth, as the suspension system had been refined pretty much to the point of pefection.

The 1995 Indy 500 was paced, once again, by a Corvette, and this prompted yet another replica. It was the third time that a Corvette had been granted this singular honor—and not the last. The 527 convertible pace car replicas were finished in Metallic Purple over Arctic White, with white hoods. The usual set of decals, which could be applied by dealers should the purchaser so specify, were supplied, plus embroidered badges on the headrests. The replica was also graced with the previously exclusive "A-mold" alloy wheels from the ZR1.

A new option to appear in 1995 was the GS-C Eagle Extended Mobility Tire (EMT). These had reinforced sidewalls that enabled the tire to run flat for up to two hundred miles, at a maximum speed of 55 mph. Bearing in mind the total noninterchangeability of the rubber on the Corvette, this was

Right: Looking like a shark in a goldfish pond, the 1995 Corvette dominates a parking lot full of European compacts.

a useful innovation and allowed for a weight-saving abandonment of the spare, for those sufficiently confident in the EMT. Road noise was a little higher with the EMT, but it was destined to become standard on all models from 1997. The lockout feature on reverse on four-speed manuals was deleted, having survived since 1959.

The passing of the ZR1 led to the introduction of an even hotter version of the 350 cu. in., cast-iron, pushrod, small-block V-8. This was the 330 bhp LT4, which was only available with manual transmission and was mandatory with the six-speed gearbox. The LT4 was a mere 45 bhp short of the output of the original LT5. A thousand "Grand Sport" versions were built, commemorating the racing Sting Rays of 1963. They were finished in Admiral Blue with a white stripe and black, or black and red, interior trim. The wheels were the ZR1's A-molds, sprayed black and fitted within bolt-on flares over the rear wheel arches, which recalled the wasp-waisted Stingray.

SPECIFICATIONS

1996
Wheelbase 96.2"
Length 14' 10"
Width 6' 2"
Weight 3,335 lb.
Transmission 4-speed auto
or 6-speed manual
Brakes 13" front
12" rear
Engine LT1 350 V-8
Compression 10.4
Net Horsepower 300

Option LT4 V-8
Compression 10.8
Net Horsepower 330

Right: The Grand Sport used ZR1-type five-spoke wheels finished in black. On the coupe they were ZR1-width with add-on flares.

Right: While the base LT1 engine remained at 300 bhp, manual cars were fitted with an LT4 rated at 330 bhp.

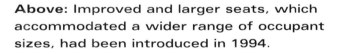

Above: Improved and larger seats, which accommodated a wider range of occupant sizes, had been introduced in 1994.

Corvette approaching another milestone.

The 1996 Sebring Silver collector's edition proved hugely popular, briefly ousting red as the preferred Corvette color. This edition also had the A-mold, five-spoke alloys but was available with either manual or automatic transmission. Various interior colors were offered, adorned with a selection of badges and embroidery.

The competition-inspired Z51 suspension option was reintroduced after a five-year layoff, and a brand new Real Time Damping (RTD) system was introduced as a replacement for the FX3 option. This was another example of overlapping Corvette technological advance, coming as it did in advance of the new C5 model. The system was incredibly complex, but highly effective and reliable.

Left: With the passing of the King, all Corvettes gained the elegant, spoked wheels that had previously been restricted to the ZR1.

Next Page: The 1996 collector's edition signaled the end of the fourth generation.

Top: The 1996 collector's edition special logos and Sebring Silver paint added $1,250 to the price sticker.

Inset: All Corvettes were luxurious by 1996. Six-way power-operated sports seats were optional (standard on the Grand Sport), trimmed with leather, naturally.

Main: Yet another commemorative edition appeared in 1996. Under the paint job, all Corvettes could be equipped with "selective real time damping" for $1,695.

1997–2006
The Best Gets Better

The king is dead . . . long live the king!

The eagerly awaited C5 series Corvette was launched in January 1997 at both the Detroit and the Los Angeles Auto Shows. A new line was to have been introduced in 1993, but due to the appalling problems that General Motors had been wrestling with in the late 1980s and early 1990s, development had been delayed and almost abandoned.

As with previous model revisions, the body shape was reworked, but this time an entirely new chassis *and* engine were introduced simultaneously—in fact, there was hardly any carryover from the previous series. That said, many features of the now departed ZR1 were to find their way into the stock Corvette. This was, naturally, the sleekest and fleetest to date, but it was also the most practical, the most comfortable, and the most economical—at least in terms of fuel consumption.

One of the perennial problems that Corvette designers and engineers had tried to address from the earliest days was producing a frame of sufficient strength and stiffness to handle the prodigious power that successive generations had been blessed with, while at the same time providing a standard of ride comfort acceptable to a domestic driver. The C5's chassis was based on a pair of extremely light but immensely strong, hydroformed rails. This design was so stiff that it could support the new Corvette's fiberglass body, even as a full convertible, with the rigidity of a standard steel sedan. The twin rail design, though expensive to put into production, eliminated the torque-flexing and scuttle shake that had plagued some previous models, notably the early, ladder-framed Makos. The effectiveness of this design was demonstrated by the fact that the coupe's Targa top could be clipped into place in seconds, rather than having to be secured with bolts at each corner as a "stressed member" providing additional stiffening to the frame, as was the case with the C4.

Ride quality was enhanced by a substantial increase in the wheelbase—up by 8 inches to 104.5 inches. This provided a more spacious interior and gave greater stability at speed. The cost of this was a slight loss of steering response, probably only noticeable to those drivers who habitually frequented mountain switchback roads. To the vast majority of owners, it represented a massive improvement in ride quality. It had been noted that the increase in the Corvette's price had been matched by an increase in its purchaser's age. The 'Vette was acknowledged to no longer be only for young boys.

Structural integrity and weight distribution were retained and improved, respectively, by the adoption of a transaxle drive system for the 4L60E automatic transmission. This placed the gearbox at the rear of the car, just ahead of the back axle. The driveshaft was encased in a "torque tube" and the auto box was given a completely redesigned, aluminum housing. Six-speed, manual transmission was available as an alternative for an additional $815. The rear-mounting of the transmission automatically provided so much additional space in the cockpit footwells that a left foot rest was deemed necessary for the driver.

The engine was still a 350, but cast in aluminum, like the ZR1's LT5, rather than formed from cast iron as was the evergreen L98/LT1. Denominated the LS1, this engine was manufactured in Romulus, Michigan, rather than in Flint, where all previous small-blocks had been assembled. It was forty-four pounds lighter than the LT1 and 45 bhp more powerful. Research had shown that the established firing order, 1-8-4-3-6-5-7-2, could induce fuel starvation from adjacent cylinders firing together. The order was therefore revised to 1-8-7-2-6-5-4-3. This produced an unfamiliar, syncopated rhythm at idle, which some owners found unacceptable and "cured" by fitting a balancer pipe between the dual exhausts. The problems caused by wet conditions and condensation to the LT1's forward-mounted distributor were cured by adopting a crankshaft trigger, with a separate coil for each spark plug.

Five-spoke, alloy wheels were standard, again recalling the ZR1. The fronts were 17 x 8 in. and the rears 18 x 9 in.; they wore Goodyear EMT tires as standard, which precluded the need to carry a spare. For European markets, however, lightweight magnesium wheels, made by Speedline of Italy, were supplied to conform with local laws. As with the ZR1 and subsequent models, provision was made for foreign detail variations in areas such as the taillights and the license plate mountings. High-intensity rear fog lights could also be provided, for areas where such things were mandatory. The Corvette was garnering foreign sales as never before—a tribute to its international reputation for both performance and reliability, which had been built up over more than forty years by a succession of talented and dedicated designers and engineers.

Right: 1997—the Corvette in its fifth incarnation. The turmoil that surrounded its gestation period is well documented in James Schefter's *All Corvettes Are Red,* published in 1997.

Opposite: Radically restyled, yet instantly recognizable. The fifth-generation Corvette represents a superb melding of tradition and innovation.

The stiff new chassis permitted an unprecedented standard of finish for the lithe new body shape. Panel fit was the best ever—always a problem with bolt-on panels, especially in GRP. The extensive employment of solid-state electronics benefited the car not only in terms of reliability, but by the fact that a vast amount of space, previously filled with cables, connectors, resistors, and regulators, was now freed up, providing yet more space for the driver and passenger. The same determination to rationalize and refine was applied to the panel work, resulting in fewer parts that simply fitted together better. Equipment levels were extremely high; the Corvette had come a long way from its spartan youth. The dashboard display now included a tire-pressure monitor and warning as standard.

SPECIFICATIONS

1997

Wheelbase 104.52"

Length 15' 0"

Width 6' 10" (including mirrors)

Weight 3,245 lb.

Transmission 4-speed auto or 6-speed manual

Brakes 13" front 12" rear

Engine LS1 350 V-8

Compression 10.0

Net Horsepower 345

Max Torque 350 lb. ft.

Above: Sleek bodywork conceals a state-of-the-art chassis.

Below: The long wheelbase and great aerodynamics make the C5 Corvette superbly stable, even at its 187 mph top speed.

Top: The entire engine compartment is styled to match the 345 hp LS5.

Bottom: At last, a Corvette with space to spare for the tallest driver.

New openings

1998 saw the arrival of a new convertible. This was a completely new design but carried styling clues from earlier series that made it an instant hit, and orders accounted for a third of total output. The soft top incorporated a glass, heated rear window and negated the need for rear fixing by employing a lever/spring tensioning system that held the rear of the roof frame tight to the deck. The roof remained, as it always had been, manually operated. Once again, a certain level of pragmatism was evident in the Corvette's design. Many would view the lack of a power roof to be an outrageous omission on a $50,000 automobile. A true Corvetteer, on the other hand, would consider the consequences of hydraulic failure during a sudden cloudburst to be more important—when else would a hydraulic failure occur?

For the fourth time, the Corvette was chosen to be the pace car for the Indianapolis 500. The color scheme for the 1998 was the wildest yet: purple with yellow wheels, a black hood, and a black and yellow leather interior. Over 1,100 were produced, at $49,464 each—making this the most expensive Corvette convertible to date.

One of the most welcome innovations of the new convertible was the provision of a trunk lid! This convenience had not been seen on a ragtop 'Vette since the early 1960s and was greeted with great enthusiasm. It even featured remote opening via a control button on the key fob.

A brand-new handling package was offered, building on the improvements introduced in earlier series: Bosch antilock braking in 1986 and ASR Traction Control in 1992. Now the JL4 Active Handling option was available for a mere $500. This system sensed any deviation from the intended cornering line by assessing and comparing the car's speed and direction against the steering angle—all this in milliseconds. By applying antilock braking to any one of the wheels, either under- or oversteer could be corrected almost imperceptibly. The system could be disabled for competition use, but for everyday driving represented yet another significant safety feature.

Right: For 1999, drivers could opt for a head-up display. Once again, aircraft technology was influencing the development of the Corvette.

1999

A hardtop 'Vette was added to the line in 1999. The idea of making this an "entry-level" model, with bargain-basement fixtures and fittings was, happily, abandoned, but it was still the cheapest route to Corvette ownership, by just under four hundred dollars. The hardtop was not removable, but bonded to the bodywork, making the car even more rigid and purposeful in feel. To underline this, six-speed, manual transmission was provided as standard, along with the upgraded Z51 suspension. Interior options and paint colors were limited, further emphasizing the hardtop's uncompromising character.

The styling of the earliest Corvettes was strongly influenced by Harley Earl's passion for aircraft design. He would have been greatly thrilled to see the introduction of a head-up display option in 1999. This employed a specially developed windshield that produced an image of the main instruments, including the digital speed indicator, directly in the driver's line of sight. The brightness and position of the display were adjustable, as was the selection of information shown. The closest experience that drivers might have had prior to this, unless they'd served as fighter pilots, would have been during the reign of the 1960s muscle cars, when a hood-mounted tacho could be specified on the Pontiac GTO.

Another feature from earlier days—Twilight Sentinel—had been featured on Cadillacs since the early 1970s. This used a photoelectric sensor to determine when the ambient light had fallen to a level that required the use of headlights, and turned the lights on accordingly. One would have thought that a Corvette owner would have been sufficiently aware of his surroundings to at least register that it was getting dark, but then again it might be handy when driving through long mountain tunnels. Twilight Sentinel was a development of a system that dated from the 1950s, which automatically dipped the lights when it sensed those of an oncoming vehicle and rejoiced in the name of the Autronic Eye.

The new millennium

Although each of the three years leading up to 2000 had seen the introduction of a new model—the C5 coupe in 1997, the convertible in 1998, and the hardtop in 1999—the only innovation offered to greet the dawn of the twenty-first century was a unique color finish: Millennium Yellow. This $500 option featured a colored lacquer layer over the base coat, which gave the finish an amazing depth and luster. Millennium Yellow recalled the color of the competition C5Rs that had acquitted themselves admirably in endurance races, notably at Daytona, Sebring, and Le Mans.

Passive keyless entry (PKE), which had been introduced in 1993, automatically unlocked or locked the doors when it sensed the approach or retreat of the key fob. It had caused a certain amount of irritation during such operations as washing the car, as it would sound the horn to indicate that doors had locked every time the owner retreated to the wash bucket or the hose. Never offered on export models, as its radio frequency might transgress local regulations, it was now deleted from the domestic options list. The wheels were restyled, with slimmer spokes, and the optional, magnesium Italian speedlines were reduced in price from a jaw-slackening $3,000 to a merely outrageous $2,000.

Above: The 2000 Corvette in its unique color finish—
Millennium Yellow.

Above: The wheel spokes of the 2000 'Vette were slimmed down to produce a lighter, more elegant look.

Top Right: Keyless entry was abandoned in 2000, along with the passenger-side key barrel.

Bottom Right: The LS1 successor to the trusty, iron small-block was forty-four pounds lighter and 45 bhp more powerful.

Right: 2001 Corvettes shared the revised engine block design of the mighty LS6, raising output to 350 bhp.

Z06

The millennium celebrations were over and so another reason to get excited was provided in the shape of the Z06 option. This was a yet more sportive development of the hardtop and was fitted with a version of the LS1 tuned to 385 bhp—more powerful than the 1992 ZR1. This was given the designation LS6, recalling the mighty 425 bhp, 427 cu. in., aluminum-headed big-block of 1971. The exterior was graced with stainless steel highlights, fully operational rear brake vents, and unique wheels that were even wider than those fitted to the coupe and the convertible, and were shod with Goodyear Eagle Supercar tires. These didn't run flat, like the EMT, and so a puncture repair kit was included in lieu of a spare. This was based on injecting a special, viscous solution into the tire and then inflating it with a canister of compressed air. The fluid automatically hardened and would plug the hole—at least long enough to get the car to a tire shop. As with the hardtop, exterior colors were limited—to black or black and red. The reworked engine block of the LS6 was fitted to the coupe and convertible also, raising their output by 5 bhp to 350 without the need for any additional tuning. Now that the hardtop had been reinvented as the Z06, it was more expensive than the coupe. The red line was put 500 rpm higher in the Z06, at 6,500 rpm. Production of both the LS1 and the LS6 was relocated to a facility in St. Catharines, Ontario, Canada.

The Corvette paced the Indy 500 for the fifth time in 2002. This was appropriate as fourteen out of the fifteen cars that completed the race were powered by Chevrolet engines—including the first three finishers. Unlike previous Indy pace car years, no replicas were offered to the public. Three cars were built as prototypes for the fiftieth anniversary model of 2003. For the statistically inclined, 2003 would be the fiftieth anniversary rather than the fifty-first as no cars were officially produced for one year between 1953 and 2003, that year being 1983.

The 2002 Z06 was rated at 405 bhp. This was achieved by the removal of two of the precatalytic converters from the exhaust system. The induction was improved and high-lift camshafts were installed, acting on a lightweight valve gear. Both intake and exhaust valves were formed hollow and were filled with potassium and sodium alloy to aid heat dispersal.

Left: In 2002, the Corvette paced the Indy 500 for the fifth time. Three pace car replicas were produced, anticipating the fiftieth anniversary model. Sadly, they were not for sale.

Fifty up

After half a century in production, the Corvette still shares its fiberglass body panels and front-engine/rear-drive layout with its 1953 forebear. While it has constantly changed, it has, in some ways, always stayed the same. There's something at once comforting and challenging about the Corvette: the older it gets, the newer it gets; fashions change but it never goes out of style. The Corvette is Forever Cool.

Fifty years of steadily increasing sales tend to indicate that those who drive Corvettes will continue to ask for more of the same and those who build Corvettes will continue to supply it. As the old saying goes, if it works, don't fix it.

Below: After half a century, the Corvette remains America's number-one performance automobile. It has fulfilled all the ambitions of 1953 by becoming one of the finest sports cars in the world.

Right: Despite its awesome complexity, the 2003 Corvette shares its GRP body panels and front-engine/rear-drive layout with the 1953 model. Some things are simply unimprovable.

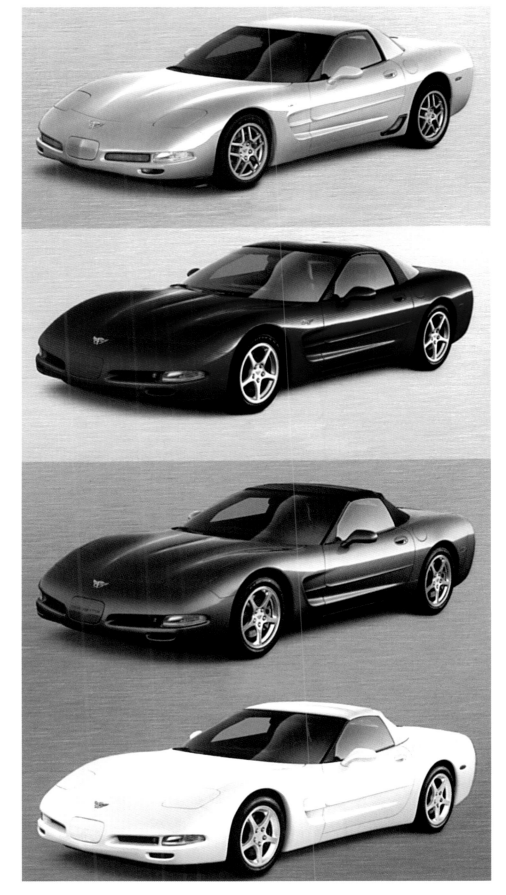

SPECIFICATIONS

2003

Wheelbase 104.52"

Length 15' 0"

Width 6' 10" (including mirrors)

Weight 3,245 lb.

Transmission 4-speed auto or 6-speed manual

Brakes 13" front 12" rear

Engine LS1 350 V-8

Compression 10.0

Net Horsepower 350

Max Torque 350 lb. ft.

Optional Z06 350 V-8

Net Horsepower 405

Max Torque 400 lb. ft.

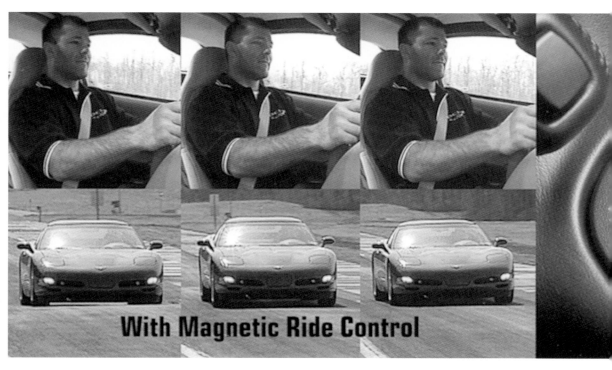

With Magnetic Ride Control

Above: New for 2003, magnetic selective ride control provides the Corvette an unparalleled level of poise and control. This sequence of pictures shows the system working on rebound as well as on compression.

Left: The special fiftieth anniversary Corvette of 2003 was available as either a coupe or a convertible, finished in Anniversary Red with gold wheels and a two-tone shale leather interior. All 2003 models featured the latest F55 Selective Magnetic Ride Control, which calculated the vertical movement of each wheel a thousand times per second.

Without Magnetic Ride Control

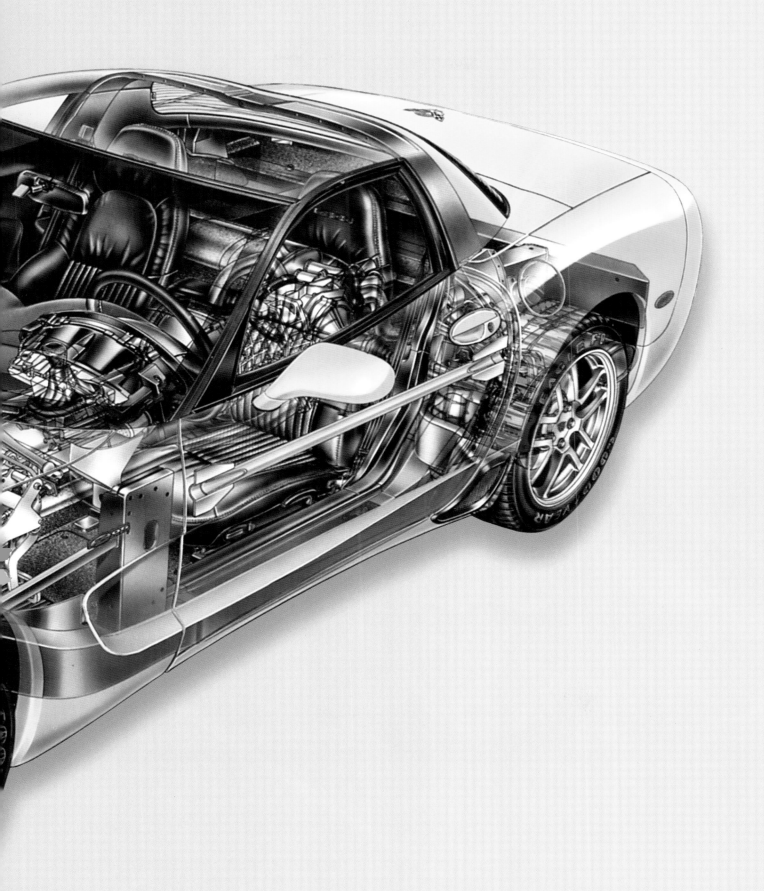

Above: What makes the Corvette a great car is what makes America a great country: power with control.

SPECIFICATIONS

2004
Wheelbase 105.52"
Length 15' 0"
Width 6' 10"
   (including mirrors)
Weight 3,215 lb.
Transmission 6-speed
   manual
Brakes 13.4" front
   13" rear
Engine LS6 350 V-8
Compression 11:1
Net Output 405 hp
Max Torque 400 lb. ft.

2004: The end of another era

The fifth-generation Corvette, having debuted in 1997 and seen the model through its fiftieth anniversary in great style, bowed out with a further brace of commemorative editions. These celebrated the consecutive GTS Class wins that Corvette Racing's C5-R's had notched up in 2001/2002 at the legendary Le Mans 24-hour race. Happily, they remained undefeated in this, their final year. The 2004 commemorative Z06 featured special Le Mans Blue color paint and a carbon fiber hood that reduced the car's weight by more than ten and a half pounds. Across the board, Z06 power output was up from 385 hp to 405 hp and the chassis was further tweaked to improve ride and handling.

The year 2004 also saw the record sixth appearance of a Corvette as the official pace car for the Indianapolis 500 at the 88th running of the race. The car used differed little from a "stock" model, but was fitted with competition-grade cooling for the power steering and transmission systems to cope with race conditions. The commemorative edition—a convertible—featured an unashamedly patriotic paint job, reflecting Chevrolet's "An American Revolution" marketing pitch.

Above: Commemorative edition Corvette coupes and convertibles shared an exclusive package of styling amenities, including Le Mans Blue paint and a shale-colored interior, with a commemorative edition exterior badge noting Corvette's Le Mans titles. Special embroidery on the headrests of each seat was also included.

Left: The 2004 commemorative edition Z06 celebrated consecutive GTS Class wins in 2001 and 2002 for the C5-R in what remains the world's most prestigious sports car endurance event—the 24 hours of Le Mans.

SPECIFICATIONS

2005
Wheelbase 106"
Length 14' 9"
Width 7' 1" (including wing mirrors)
Weight 3,176 lb.
Transmission Hydra-Matic 4L65-E 4-speed auto, Tremec 6-speed manual
Brakes 13" front
        12" rear
Engine LS2 V-8
Compression 10.9:1
Net Output 400 hp
Max Torque 400 lb. ft.

C6—The theory of evolution

When the C5 was introduced in 1997, it had little in common with its predecessor. Its replacement, however, draws heavily on the C5's design and componentry, but prospective purchasers shouldn't worry that they're getting little more than a restyle. The C6 Corvette is the best yet: well worth the money and well worth waiting for.

The sixth-generation Corvette is a little shorter and slimmer overall but rides a wheelbase that is actually longer by about an inch and a quarter. Weight is almost unchanged but power output is increased by 50 hp with a substantial increase in torque, particularly via the reworked 4L65-E auto box, which now features Performance Algorithm Shifting to allow even more spirited fast driving on twisting roads. Synchromesh on the six-speed manual transmission has been improved to allow for quicker and slicker changes. Cylinder bore has been increased from 3.9 inches to 4, raising displacement by 305 cc. Subtle resculpturing of the

Right: The C6 interior features cast-skin, leather-effect safety coverings for the instrument panel and doors. Seats have adjustable lumbar support as well as head and torso protection via side-impact airbags. Instrument lighting and Driver Information Center readouts are provided via organic light-emitting diodes. The optional head-up display now features street and competition modes.

Left: The 2005 C6—the sixth-generation Corvette—delivers, in GM's own words, "more power, passion and precision to reach a new standard of performance car excellence." You could add that it also sets new standards in safety and efficiency. The C6 is truly *the* performance car for the twenty-first century *and* you can see the headlights.

SPECIFICATIONS

2005
Wheelbase 106"
Length 14' 9"
Width 7' 1" (including
  mirrors)
Weight 3,179 lb.
Transmission Hydra-Matic
  4L65-E 4-speed auto
  Tremec 6-speed manual
Brakes 13" front
  12" rear
Engine LS2 V-8
Compression 10.9:1
Net Output 400 hp
Max Torque 400 lb. ft.

Above: The manual gearshift and door releases are accented with anodized aluminum that is specially screen printed to reduce reflection and resist marking. The twin-cockpit layout—a Corvette speciality—is still retained, though the grab-handle is gone in favor of a more effective passenger airbag.

body has given the C6 an incredibly low .28 coefficient of drag, down fractionally from the already slippery C5.

Two optional suspension packages are available as alternatives to the standard setup, which provides an excellent combination of smooth ride and taut handling. The F55 Magnetic Selective Ride Control system was introduced on the 2003 fiftieth anniversary edition car. It provides effectively instantaneous adjustment to the damping by using a magneto-rheological fluid (whose viscosity is varied by electronic impulses) to optimize driver control and comfort. On the C6, two settings allow for standard touring and for sport driving. The Z51 package brings the C6 coupe's performance close to that of the Z06 via the incorporation of extra-heavy-duty springs, dampers, and stabilizer bars, plus larger, cross-drilled brake discs.

Inside, the ambience is familiar but has been subtly refined. The optional head-up display now has two modes: street and track, the latter showing the level of G-Force generated during cornering. For the first

time, the OnStar system is offered (as an option) as well. A full compliment of airbags is fitted and seat heaters are available for those who like the idea of a little localized global warming.

With a kerb weight of around 3,250 lbs. and a maximum power output of 400 @ 6,000 rpm, the C6 in guaranteed to go as fast as most people would want—maybe even a little faster—but those who rail against "excessive" automobile performance should bear in mind that all things are relative. The C6 Corvette has even larger brake discs than its predecessor and extended mobility 245/40ZR-18 Goodyear Eagle F1 tires previously reserved for the Z06. The C6 Corvette's safety and handling are concomitant with the car's power and performance. Whatever speed the new Corvette—or any Corvette for that matter—is driven at, the level of safety and performance remains the same— very high. Fuel economy, for an automobile with such stupendous performance, is remarkable. Overall, the C6 Corvette delivers 22.6 miles per gallon. Compare that to the marginally more expensive Ferrari

Above: Even with its exposed headlights, the 2005 C6 convertible is recognizable as a Corvette at fifty paces—that's breeding for you. Though advanced CAD techniques are employed throughout the design process, traditional hand-sculpting is still used to produce what can only be described as poetry in motion.

SPECIFICATIONS

2006 Z06
Wheelbase 106"
Length 14' 9"
Width 7' 4" (including mirrors)
Weight 3,130 lb.
Transmission Tremec 6-speed manual
Brakes 14" front 13.4" rear
Engine LS7 V-8
Compression 11:1
Net Output 500 hp
Max Torque 475 lb. ft.

Above: Lightweight seats are specially shaped to keep the driver firmly in place, since the Z06 can generate fighter-plane G forces in fast bends. The unique instrument cluster reflects the car's competition lineage, having been developed alongside the awesome Le Mans–winning C5-R race cars.

Modena which, with the same power output, manages a much less impressive 12.7 mpg.

Unlike the C5, the C6 features a fully functioning radiator grille and this is surmounted—can it be?—by exposed headlights! Not since 1962 have we seen a Corvette's headlights when they were switched off, but it must be assumed that a "fixed" headlight system allows for more accurate alignment, particularly over time and rough roads. Each enclosed mounting contains an HID (high-intensity discharge) Xenon low-beam lens, an HID Xenon high-beam lens, and a turn indicator. The power of the illumination of these lights is in keeping with the C6's performance.

Dave Hill, Corvette's chief engineer, has stated, "Our goal is to create a Corvette that does more things well than any other performance car." He and his team seem to be doing pretty well.

Above: The C6 Z06 debuts at the North American show. This is the fastest and most powerful automobile ever offered by Chevrolet, delivering 500 hp and 475 lb. ft. of torque. Kerb weight is a little over 3,000 lbs. The LS7 engines are assembled by hand at GM's state-of-the-art Performance Build Center.

Z06—Still not satisfied?

The 2006 Z06 is simply the fastest, most powerful Corvette ever built. It produces 500 horsepower at 6200 rpm and 475 lb. ft. of torque. The 427 ci LS7 V8 motor incorporates titanium con-rods and inlet valves and dry-sump lubrication. The body is crafted from aluminum, with carbon-fiber front fenders and hood. The one-piece perimeter chassis is made of hydroformed aluminum, giving a kerb weight of 3,130 lbs. The 0–60 acceleration is well inside four seconds and, to save upsetting those of a nervous disposition, let's say that the top speed of the 2006 Z06 will be in the region of what a Roman would term CC. The race may not always be to the swiftest. But it helps.

CORVETTE TIME LINE 1953–2005

1953

June 30. The first Corvette comes off the line at Flint, Michigan. Like all the first batch, it is a Polo White Roadster with Sportsman Red interior. Transmission is via two-speed Powerglide. 0–60 = 11.0 sec. Top speed = 106 mph.

Dwight D. Eisenhower is sworn in as 34th President of the United States.

Elizabeth II is crowned Queen of England.

Hugh Heffner publishes the first *Playboy* magazine.

Ray Bradbury publishes *Fahrenheit 451*.

L. Ron Hubbard founds the Church of Scientology.

IBM introduces its first computer, the 701, with a capacity of 4 kb.

Edmund Hilary and Sherpa Norkey Tenzing reach the summit of Everest.

Crick and Watson discover the double helix structure of DNA.

Ben Hogan wins the U.S. Open, the Masters, and the British Open, becoming the first golfer to win three majors in one year.

The New York Yankees beat the Brooklyn Dodgers and become the first team to win the World Series five times in a row.

Josef Stalin dies.

Hank Williams dies.

Kim Basinger is born.

Tony Blair is born.

1954

Corvette production is switched to St. Louis, Missouri, where output reaches 600 cars a month, outstripping demand. The Corvette is now available in Pennant Blue and Sportsman Red as well as Polo White.

The fifty-millionth automobile to be built by an American manufacturer comes off the line, at Flint, Michigan—it's a Chevrolet.

The Mercedes-Benz 300 SL is the first car to feature fuel injection.

A study reveals that 80 percent of atmospheric pollution in the greater Los Angeles area of California is caused by automobiles.

The U.S. National Cancer Institute links tobacco smoking to lung cancer.

America's first atomic power plant is built in Pittsburgh, Pennsylvania.

French troops surrender at Dien Bien Phu.

Marlon Brando stars in *The Wild One*.

J. R. R. Tolkien publishes *The Fellowship of the Ring*.

Marilyn Monroe marries Joe DiMaggio.

Marilyn Monroe sues for divorce.

Henri Matisse dies.

John Travolta is born.

1955

The Corvette is supplied with a 265 cid, overhead-valve V-8, producing 195 bhp. New colors include Harvest Gold and Metallic Copper. 0–60 = 8.5 sec. Top speed = 115 mph. Only 674 cars are sold.

Marian Anderson becomes the first black singer to perform at the Metropolitan Opera House, New York.

Bill Haley and the Comets release *Rock Around the Clock*.

Chuck Berry releases *Maybelline*.

James Dean stars in *Rebel Without a Cause*.

J. R. R. Tolkien publishes *The Two Towers*.

Disneyland, the first theme park in the world, opens in Anaheim, California.

Lassie appears on U.S. television for the first time, along with *Champion, the Wonder Horse* and *The Phil Silvers Show*.

The United States Auto Club replaces the American Automobile Association as the governing body for Indy-car racing.

Louison Bobet of France becomes the first man to win the Tour de France three years in succession.

Willie Shoemaker wins his fifth Kentucky Derby, on Swaps.

Albert Einstein dies.

Charlie "Bird" Parker dies.

Kevin Costner is born.

Bill Gates in born.

1956

The Corvette is dramatically restyled and fitted with a close-ratio, three-speed, manual gearbox. The V-8's output is increased to 225 bhp. 0–60 = 7.5 sec. Top speed = 120 mph. Sales leap to 3,467.

Dwight D. Eisenhower is reelected President of the United States.

Fidel Castro lands in Cuba.

Felix Wankel invents the rotary engine.

The U.S. Congress passes the Federal Aid Highway Act, permitting the construction of 42,500 miles of interstate highway, to be funded by a tax on gasoline.

The General Motors Technical Center opens in Warren, Michigan.

Maria Callas debuts at the Metropolitan Opera House, New York.

Marilyn Monroe marries Arthur Miller.

Grace Kelly marries Prince Rainier of Monaco.

Yul Brenner stars in *The King and I*.

J. R. R. Tolkien publishes *The Return of the King*.

Elvis Presley releases *Hound Dog*.

Doris Day releases *Que Sera, Sera*.

William E. Boeing dies.

Tom Hanks is born.

1957

The Corvette gets "Ramjet" fuel-injection and four-speed, manual transmission. Bored out to 283 cid, the V-8's power output is increased to a maximum of 283 bhp. 0–60 = 5.7 sec. Top speed = 132 mph.

President Dwight D. Eisenhower is inaugurated for a second term and the public ceremonies are videotaped and become the first nationally broadcast item.

The U.S.S.R. launches *Sputnik I*, the world's first artificial satellite.

Evangelist Billy Graham concludes a four-month tour of the United States.

Juan Manuel Fangio becomes the first man to be Formula One World Champion four times in a row.

Althea Gibson of the United States becomes the first black player to win a singles title at the Wimbledon Lawn Tennis championships in England.

Sony produces the first miniature transistor radio.

Smith-Corona produces the first portable electric typewriter.

Henry Fonda stars in *Twelve Angry Men*.

Grant Williams stars in *The Incredible Shrinking Man*.

Ian Fleming publishes *From Russia with Love*.

Boris Pasternak publishes *Doctor Zhivago*.

The Everly Brothers release *Bye Bye Love*.

Senator Joe McCarthy and Eliot Ness die.

Humphrey Bogart dies.

Seve Ballesteros and Nick Faldo are born.

1958

Corvette fuel-injected horsepower reaches 290 and so exceeds 1 hp per cubic inch. Sales and chromium increase proportionally. Entry-level price is kept low at $3,631, but the model shows a profit for the first time.

Bank Americard is launched, the first true credit card.

Chairman Mao instigates China's "Great Leap Forward."

The National Aeronautics and Space Administration (NASA) is created.

National Airlines introduces the first nonstop service between New York and Miami.

Bell Laboratories produces the first modem, which permits a telephone line to carry information in binary form and is the first step to creating the World Wide Web.

American Jack Kilby demonstrates the first integrated circuit. It consists of a silicone substrate containing transistors, resistors, and capacitors and leads to the third generation of computers.

Steve McQueen stars in *The Blob*.

Maurice Chevalier and Leslie Caron star in *Gigi*.

Perry Como releases *Magic Moments*.

Elvis Presley begins two years of military service.

Pope Pius XII dies.

Tyrone Power dies.

Michelle Pfieffer is born.

Michael Jackson is born.

1959

1960

Harley Earl, father of the Corvette, retires as head of styling at General Motors. Chromium trim is deleted and rear suspension is revised to cope with ever-increasing power output.

Alaska becomes the 49th state and Hawaii becomes the 50th state.

Oklahoma repeals prohibition.

Soviet leader Nikita Krushchev visits the United States.

The U.S. Navy launches *Vanguard 2*, the world's first weather satellite.

The Guggenheim Museum, designed by Frank Lloyd Wright, opens in New York.

Ed Wood Jr.'s *Plan Nine from Outer Space* is released.

Ian Fleming publishes *Goldfinger*.

Bobby Darin releases *Mack the Knife*.

The Barbie doll goes on sale.

Rawhide appears on U.S. TV for the first time, featuring Clint Eastwood.

The Untouchables appears on U.S. TV for the first time, starring Robert Stack.

Ingemar Johansson knocks out Floyd Patterson to become heavyweight champion of the world.

Lee Petty, driving an Oldsmobile 88, wins the inaugural Daytona 500.

C. B. De Mille, Buddy Holly, Raymond Chandler, Errol Flynn, General George C. Marshall, and Frank Lloyd Wright die.

John McEnroe is born.

Corvette production exceeds 10,000 for the first time. Compression on top fuel-injected models rises to 11:1. Maximum output is now 315 bhp. Options include a 24-gallon fuel tank and competition suspension. The Corvette dominates sports car racing as Briggs Cunningham's team places eighth at Le Mans.

Chrysler discontinues the De Soto line after 42 years of production.

The Organization of Petroleum Exporting Countries (OPEC) meets for the first time, in Iraq, and raises the price of oil.

The United States imposes an export embargo on Cuba.

John F. Kennedy is elected president by the narrowest margin in history, defeating Richard M. Nixon by a tenth of a percent.

The State of California approves the U.S.'s first antismog legislation.

Paul Newman and Eve Marie Saint star in *Exodus*.

Anthony Perkins, Vera Miles, and Janet Leigh star in *Psycho*.

The Beatles release *She Loves You*.

Elvis Presley releases *Are You Lonesome Tonight?*

Harper Lee publishes *To Kill a Mockingbird*.

The U.S. flag gets fifty stars.

Floyd Patterson regains the world heavyweight boxing championship by defeating Ingemar Johansson.

Cassius Clay wins the light-heavyweight boxing gold medal at the Olympic Games in Rome.

John D. Rockefeller dies.

Ayrton Senna is born.

1961

The Corvette's tail and radiator grille are restyled. Fuel-injected cars can run 0–60 mph in 5.5 seconds and have a top speed in excess of 130 mph.

Adolf Eichmann is tried in Israel for war crimes, convicted, and sentenced to death.

John F. Kennedy is sworn in as 35th—and youngest ever—U.S. President.

The Bay of Pigs invasion by U.S.-trained Cuban exiles fails.

The first American troops land in Vietnam.

IBM introduces the electronic "Golf Ball" typewriter.

Mattel Toys launches Ken, a boyfriend for Barbie.

Alan Sheppard becomes the first U.S. astronaut in space.

Edward Lorenz comes up with the Chaos Theory.

Charlton Heston and Sophia Loren star in *El Cid*.

Clark Gable, Marilyn Monroe, and Montgomery Clift star in *The Misfits*.

Yevgeny Yevtushenko publishes his poem *Babi Yar*.

Joseph Heller publishes his novel *Catch-22*.

Bobby Vee releases *Poetry in Motion*.

The Dick Van Dyke Show appears on U.S. TV for the first time.

Dr. Kildare appears on U.S. TV for the first time, starring Richard Chamberlain.

Ernest Hemingway commits suicide.

Lady Diana Spencer (later Princess Diana) is born.

1962

Corvette 283 cid engines are bored out to 327 cid. Maximum power output rises to 360 bhp. Two-tone accenting on the side coves is deleted. Dick Thompson, "the Flying Dentist," wins the SCCA A-Production title in a Corvette. Production increases to 14,500.

The U.S. national debt passes the $300 billion mark.

U2 pilot Gary Powers is released by the Russians in exchange for Soviet spy Rudolf Abel.

Nelson Mandela is sentenced to five years imprisonment in South Africa for inciting workers to strike.

The Cuban missile crisis brings the U.S. and U.S.S.R. close to war.

Telstar, the first U.S. telecommunications satellite, is launched.

Dr. No, the first James Bond movie, directed by Terence Young, is released.

How the West Was Won, directed by John Ford, is released.

Anthony Burgess's *A Clockwork Orange* is published.

Ken Kesey's *One Flew Over the Cuckoo's Nest* is published.

Bob Dylan releases *Blowin' in the Wind*.

The Beach Boys release *Surfin' Safari*.

Philip Morris introduces the Marlboro cowboy.

The Beverley Hillbillies appears on U.S. TV for the first time.

Sonny Liston defeats Floyd Patterson to become heavyweight boxing champion of the world.

Marilyn Monroe dies.

Jodie Foster is born.

1963

The second generation. Bill Mitchell's Corvette Sting Ray is introduced, with a new, ladder-frame chassis designed by Zora Arkus-Duntov. The radically restyled new model is shorter, narrower, and lighter than its predecessor. The divided rear window of the new coupe proves controversial. The first Z06 package is offered. Sales double.

Martin Luther King Jr. addresses around two hundred thousand people in Washington D.C., delivering the famous "I have a dream" speech.

President John F. Kennedy addresses around two hundred thousand people in West Berlin, delivering the famous "Ich bin ein Berliner" speech.

Frank Sinatra Jr. is kidnapped in Lake Tahoe, Nevada, and ransomed for a quarter of a million dollars, which is paid by his father.

The United States now has six percent of the world's population and 66 percent of the world's automobiles.

Kodak introduces the first Instamatic camera.

Sean Connery stars as James Bond in *From Russia with Love.*

The Beatles release *Please Please Me.*

Frank Sinatra releases *Fly Me to the Moon.*

The Fugitive, starring David Janssen, appears on U.S. TV for the first time.

Arnold Palmer becomes the first golfer to win over a million dollars in a season.

The Chicago Bears win a record seventh NFL title.

President John F. Kennedy is assassinated in Dallas, Texas.

1964

The Corvette Sting Ray loses its fake hood louvers. Top power for the fuelie rises to 375 bhp. Coupe rear window divide is deleted. Options now include leather upholstery, power steering, power brakes, air-conditioning, and stereo.

Lyndon B. Johnson is now the 36th President of the United States.

U.S. warships are attacked off the coast of North Vietnam.

Martin Luther King Jr. wins the Nobel Prize for Peace.

The Varrazano-Narrows suspension bridge, between Staten Island and Brooklyn, is opened. It has the longest single span in the world, at 4,258 ft.

Stanley Kubrick's *Dr. Strangelove, or How I Learned to Stop Worrying and Love the Bomb*, is released.

George Cukor's *My Fair Lady* is released.

Richard Burton and Elizabeth Taylor marry in Montreal, Canada.

Both the Chrysler Corporation and the Ford Motor Corporation succeed in signing deals with the UAW, but GM fails and production is severely disrupted by strikes.

The Addams Family appear on U.S. TV for the first time.

The Man from U.N.C.L.E. appears on U.S. TV for the first time.

Cassius Clay defeats Sonny Liston to become the heavyweight boxing champion of the world. Clay then converts to Islam and changes his name to Muhammad Ali.

Englishman Donald Campbell becomes the first man to hold both the world's land speed and water speed records.

General Douglas MacArthur, Herbert Hoover, and Cole Porter die.

Keanu Reeves is born.

1965

Roger Penske takes a class win in a Corvette at Nassau. The big-block V-8 is introduced, initially at 396 cid, later 427 cid. Clutch, cooling, and suspension are all upgraded to deal with the 425 bhp output.

Malcolm X is shot dead in New York.

Race riots erupt in the Watts district of Los Angeles, California.

U.S. soldiers enter the war in Vietnam for the first time at Danang.

U.S. aircraft bomb North Vietnam in Operation Rolling Thunder.

Congress orders that all cigarette packets sold in the U.S. must carry a health warning.

The Highway Beautification Act bans roadside advertising.

Ralph Nader publishes *Unsafe at any Speed*.

David Lean's *Doctor Zhivago* is released.

Robert Wise's *The Sound of Music* is released.

Bob Dylan plays electric guitar at the Newport Folk Festival.

Pope Paul VI celebrates mass at Yankee Stadium.

Timothy Leary coins the phrase "Turn on, tune in, drop out."

Allan Ginsberg coins the expression "flower power."

Riding an MV Agusta, English motorcyclist Mike Hailwood wins his fourth successive 500 cc world championship.

Driving a Lotus, Scottish racing driver Jim Clark is the first European to win the Indianapolis 500 since Louis Chevrolet in 1920.

Winston Churchill, Albert Schweitzer, and Adlai Stevenson die.

Bjork is born.

1966

A 427 cid, Corvette Mark IV can hit 60 mph in under five seconds and has a top speed of over 140 mph. Sales approach 28,000.

LSD is declared illegal in the United States.

U.S. troops in Vietnam number over 400,000.

The minimum wage is increased from $1.25 to $1.40 per hour.

The U.S. coastal fishing limit is increased from three to twelve miles.

Clint Eastwood and Lee Van Cleef star in *The Good, the Bad, and the Ugly*.

Lee Marvis wins the Academy Award for best actor for *Cat Ballou*.

Frank Sinatra sings *Strangers in the Night*.

Nancy Sinatra sings *These Boots Are Made for Walkin'*.

John Lennon opines that the Beatles are more popular than Jesus.

The Monkees are created.

Batman appears on U.S. TV for the first time.

Tarzan appears on U.S. TV for the first time.

England beats West Germany to win the soccer world cup at Wembley, England.

Muhammad Ali beats Cleveland Williams to retain the world heavyweight boxing championship.

Walt Disney dies.

Janet Jackson is born.

1967

Introduction of the new Corvette is delayed due to development problems, allowing the Sting Ray to enjoy an "Indian summer." Embellishment is reduced to zero. The Corvette never looked better.

Expo '76 opens in Montreal, Canada.

The Six Day War begins and ends in victory for Israel.

Virgil Grissom, Edward White, and Roger Chaffee become the first fatalities of the U.S. space program in *Apollo 1*.

Vladimir Komarov becomes the first fatality of the U.S.S.R. space program, in *Soyuz 1*.

Dr. Christiaan Barnard performs the first heart transplant operation, in South Africa.

Dr. Adrian Kantrowitz performs the first heart transplant operation in the U.S.

The first domestic microwave oven goes on sale in the U.S.

Mazda of Japan produces the first rotary-engined car.

The liner *Queen Elizabeth II* is launched on the River Clyde, Scotland.

Warren Beatty and Faye Dunaway star in *Bonnie and Clyde*.

Dustin Hoffman and Anne Bancroft star in *The Graduate*.

John Boorman directs *Point Blank*.

The Beatles release *Sgt. Peppers Lonely Hearts Club Band*.

The Jimi Hendrix Experience releases *Are You Experienced?*

Che Guevara dies.

Kurt Cobain is born.

1968

The third-generation Corvette is announced and is branded "unfit to test" by one reviewer. Its striking appearance is marred by poor quality control. Despite the criticisms, sales reach an all-time high of 28,500.

The United Auto Workers Union mergers with the Teamsters to form the Alliance for Labor Action.

Feminists demonstrate against the Miss America pageant in Atlantic City, New Jersey.

Lyndon B. Johnson orders the cessation of the bombing of North Vietnam.

Stanley Kubrik's *2001: A Space Odyssey* is released.

Peter Yate's *Bullitt* is released.

The 911 emergency telephone service is introduced.

The Jacuzzi Brothers introduce their first "whirlpool bath."

Rowan and Martin's Laugh-In appears on U.S. television.

U.S. athletes Tommie Smith and John Carlos give "black power" salutes from the winners' podium of the Olympic Games in Mexico City.

Muhammad Ali is stripped of his world heavyweight boxing title for refusing to be drafted into the army.

Martin Luther King Jr. is assassinated in Memphis, Tennessee.

Robert Kennedy is assassinated in Los Angeles, California.

Yuri Gagarin, the first man in space, dies in an jet plane crash near Moscow.

Jim Clark, world champion racing driver, dies in a race car crash at Hockenheim.

1969

The Stingray name is reintroduced, as one word. Much work is done to correct design flaws and increase cockpit space. Emission control prompts the lowering of compression ratios. The 250,000th Corvette is produced at St. Louis, Missouri.

Richard M. Nixon is sworn in as 37th President of the U.S.

Senator Edward Kennedy drives off a bridge at Cappaquiddick Island. His passenger, Mary Jo Kopechne, drowns.

Apollo 11 lands on the moon and Neil Armstrong says, "One small step for a man, one giant leap for mankind."

Charles Manson and his followers murder actress Sharon Tate and others at the home of her husband, film director Roman Polanski, in Bel Air, California.

Dennis Hopper's *Easy Rider* is released.

George Roy Hill's *Butch Cassidy and the Sundance Kid* is released.

Mario Puzo publishes *The Godfather*.

Kurt Vonnegut publishes *Slaughterhouse-Five*.

Frank Sinatra releases *My Way*.

Leonard Cohen releases *Songs from a Room*.

500,000 people go to listen to the music at Woodstock.

Hell's Angels kill a fan at Altamont.

Penthouse goes on sale for the first time.

Sesame Street goes on TV for the first time.

Dwight Eisenhower, Ho Chi Minh, and Judy Garland die.

Sean "P. Diddy" Combs is born.

1970

Corvette production drops by half due to a prolonged autoworkers strike. To compensate for the drop in compression ratios, the big-block engine gets even bigger, up to 454 cu. in. The solid-lifter, 370 bhp, LT1 version of the small-block is introduced. Design details continue to be revised and refined.

U.S. troop withdrawals from Vietnam continue. 150,000 U.S. service personnel come home.

The National Guard fires on student demonstrators at Kent State University, Ohio, killing four.

IBM introduces the "floppy disk" for computer data storage.

Canon Business Systems produces the first pocket calculator.

The U.S. military initiates the GPS (Global Positioning System) for navigation, utilizing twenty-one satellites.

The north tower of the World Trade Center in New York is completed. At 1,350 ft., it is the tallest building on earth.

M.A.S.H. wins the Palme d'Or at the Cannes Film Festival.

John Wayne wins the best actor Oscar for *True Grit*.

Simon and Garfunkel release *Bridge Over Troubled Water*.

Richard Bach publishes *Jonathan Livingston Seagull*.

Cigarette advertising is banned on radio and TV in the U.S.

Joe Frazier becomes the undisputed heavyweight champion of the world.

Gary Gabelich takes the world land speed record in his *Blue Flame* rocket-powered car at Bonneville Salt Flats, Utah.

Jimi Hendrix dies.

River Phoenix is born.

1971

Corvette sales rise to 21,801, having fallen well below 20,000 in the previous year. Economic uncertainty, emission legislation, rising gasoline prices, and insurance premiums all conspire against the manufacture and sale of high-performance cars.

The twenty-sixth amendment to the Constitution gives the vote to eighteen-year-olds.

The environmental protest group Greenpeace is founded.

An earthquake kills fifty-one people in Los Angeles.

Tornadoes kill over 100 people in Mississippi and Louisiana.

Floods kill more than 100,000 people in North Vietnam.

Quadraphonic stereo is introduced.

Rolls Royce Motors goes bankrupt.

Stanley Kubrick's *A Clockwork Orange* is released.

Peter Bogdanovitch's *The Last Picture Show* is released.

Stephen Spielberg's TV movie *Duel* is broadcast.

Disney World opens in Orlando, Florida.

Joe Frazier beats Muhammad Ali to retain his world heavyweight boxing title.

A U.S. table tennis team plays a series of matches in the People's Republic of China.

Al Unser wins his second Indy 500 at an average speed of over 157 mph.

The L.A. Lakers set a record of twenty-seven straight wins.

Louis Armstrong, Jim Morrison, and Igor Stravinsky die.

Pete Sampras is born.

1972

Horsepower ratings are switched from gross to net (SAE), which made them seem even lower, thus the output of 1972's most powerful engine appears to be equal to 1971's least powerful, at 270 bhp. The LS6 engine option is deleted.

The U.S.S.R. begins bulk purchase of surplus grain from the U.S.

Governor George Wallace is shot and paralyzed at a political meeting in Maryland.

Bob Woodward and Carl Bernstein of the *Washington Post* report a break-in at the Democratic Party Headquarters in the Watergate Hotel complex, Washington, D.C.

Polaroid introduces the SX-70, their first color camera.

Federal Express is founded.

Marlon Brando stars in *The Godfather*.

Gene Hackman stars in *The Poseidon Adventure*.

Lisa Minelli stars in *Cabaret*.

The Waltons first appears on U.S. TV.

British racing driver Graham Hill becomes the first person to have won the Formula 1 World Championship, the Indianapolis 500, and the Le Mans 24-hour race.

U.S. Golfer Jack Nicklaus wins his third U.S. Open.

U.S. swimmer Mark Spitz wins seven gold medals at the Munich Olympic Games.

Eleven Israeli athletes are murdered by Arab terrorists at the Munich Olympic Games.

J. Edgar Hoover, Charles Atlas, King Edward VIII, and Maurice Chevalier die.

1973

The Corvette gets an impact-resistant "soft nose" and improvements to the chassis mounts. Engine options are reduced to two 350s and one 454. Sales climb back above 30,000.

Richard Milhous Nixon is sworn in for a second term as president.

OPEC announces a doubling in the price of oil.

The last U.S. troops are evacuated from Vietnam.

U.S. Secretary of State Henry Kissinger and founding member of the Indochinese Communist Party, Le Duc Tho, share the Nobel Peace Prize.

Egypt and Syria attack Israel on the Jewish holy day of Yom Kippur.

The U.S. agrees to grant two billion dollars worth of military aid to Israel.

The Sears Tower is Chicago, Illinois, becomes the world's tallest building at 1,454 ft. The World Trade Center in New York is completed.

George Lucas's *American Graffiti* is released.

William Friedkin's *The Exorcist* is released.

Elton John releases *Goodbye, Yellow Brick Road*.

George Foreman defeats Joe Frazier to become world heavyweight boxing champion.

O. J. Simpson of the Buffalo Bills becomes the first football player to gain more than 2,000 yards rushing in a season.

Lyndon B. Johnson and Edward G. Robinson die.

1974

Zora Arkus-Duntov retires. The LT1 and the big-block engine options are deleted. The Corvette gets an impact-absorbing tail section to match its "soft" nose. Times are tough for sports cars but Corvette sales climb steadily.

President Richard M. Nixon resigns to avoid impeachment over the Watergate affair.

Gerald Rudolph Ford is sworn in as the 38th President of the United States.

Brazil introduces a new automobile fuel, known as *alcool*, a mixture of gasoline and ethyl alcohol distilled from sugar.

The Arab oil embargo against the United States is lifted.

The first bar codes appear in U.S. supermarkets.

Robert Redford stars in *The Great Gatsby*.

Jack Nicholson stars in *Chinatown*.

Robert M. Pirsig publishes *Zen and the Art of Motorcycle Maintenance*.

Happy Days appears on U.S. TV.

Hank Aaron of the Atlanta Braves tops Babe Ruth's record of 714 home runs, which had stood since 1935.

Belgian cyclist Eddy Merckx becomes the first rider to win the Tour de France, the Giro d'Italia, and the World Road Race Championship in the same season.

Muhammad Ali defeats George Foreman to regain the world heavyweight boxing title.

Girls are permitted to play baseball in the Little League for the first time.

Errett Lobban Cord dies.

1975

1976

Dave McLellan becomes Corvette chief engineer and vows to retain the traditional front-engine, rear-drive layout, although much time, effort, and money has been spent on experimental, mid-engined prototypes. The Corvette remains virtually unchanged, as do sales, though they now approach 40,000.

GM is overtaken by Exxon (formerly Standard Oil) as America's richest company.

Bill Gates founds Microsoft.

Staff are evacuated by helicopter from the roof of the U.S. Embassy in Saigon.

Two assassination attempts are made against President Ford.

The Suez Canal reopens.

Liquid crystal displays (LCDs) appear.

Jimmy Hoffa disappears.

The first drive-through McDonald's opens.

Over a quarter of a million U.S. autoworkers are laid off.

Steven Spielberg's *Jaws* is released.

Jim Sharman's *The Rocky Horror Picture Show* is released.

Saturday Night Live appears on U.S. TV.

Billie Jean King wins the ladies singles tennis championship at Wimbledon.

Arthur Ashe wins the men's singles tennis championship at Wimbledon.

Aristotle Onassis, second husband of Jackie Kennedy, dies.

Graham Hill dies.

In the bicentennial year, there is no Corvette roadster for the first time since the model was introduced in 1953 and, at the end of the year, the Stingray name was finally abandoned. Sales rise to over 46,500.

Vietnam is reunified.

Israeli special forces rescue over a hundred hijacked hostages from Entebbe, Uganda.

The U.S. *Viking* spacecraft land on Mars.

The Concorde supersonic airliner enters service.

A Lockheed "Blackbird" sets a jet speed record of over 2,000 miles per hour.

Alex Haley publishes *Roots*.

The Eagles release *Hotel California*.

Sony introduces the Betamax video-cassette recorder.

JVC introduce the VHS video-cassette recorder.

Charlie's Angels appears on U.S. TV for the first time.

Laverne & Shirley appears on U.S. TV for the first time.

Twenty-nine members of the American Legion die of an unknown illness contracted at a congress in Philadelphia. The infection is dubbed Legionnaire's Disease.

Austrian driver Nikki Lauda is severely injured in a crash at the German Grand Prix.

Sissy Spacek stars in *Carrie*.

Sylvester Stallone stars in *Rocky*.

John Paul Getty and Mao Tse Tung die.

1977

Bill Mitchell retires and the mid-engined Aerovette concept is quietly shelved. Rotary motors have been tried and found wanting; the 350 small-block soldiers on and sales come close to 50,000.

Jimmy Carter is sworn in as the 39th President of the United States.

Apple launches the first personal computer.

New York experiences a twenty-four-hour power cut.

California makes the fitting of catalytic exhaust converters to all new automobiles mandatory.

Laker Airways provides a New York–London round-trip service for $100.00.

Close Encounters of the Third Kind is released.

Saturday Night Fever is released.

Star Wars is released.

Fleetwood Mac releases *Rumors*.

Meat Loaf releases *Bat Out of Hell*.

Alex Haley's *Roots* is shown over eight nights on U.S. TV.

The Love Boat appears on U.S. TV for the first time.

A. J. Foyt becomes the first driver to win the Indy 500 four times.

Jockey Steve Cauthen makes over six million dollars prize money in his first season.

Charlie Chaplin dies.

Elvis Presley, Bing Crosby, and Maria Callas die.

1978

The Corvette, celebrating its twenty-fifth birthday, gets a completely new, wraparound, rear window treatment.
A commemorative silver anniversary edition is produced, plus an Indy pace car replica.

Ben Cohen and Jerry Greenfield open an ice-cream parlor in Vermont.

The dollar rises sharply after U.S. President Jimmy Carter announces a major support plan, including higher interest rates.

Cleveland, Ohio, defaults on its debts, the first U.S. city to do so since the 1930s depression.

The Ford Motor Corporation is fined over a hundred million in lawsuits over a flawed filler-neck and fuel tank design.

CFCs, gases used as propellants in aerosols, are banned in the U.S.

Apple unveils personal computers with disk drives.

The first "test tube" baby is born in London, England.

John Irving publishes *The World According to Garp*.

Robert De Niro stars in *The Deer Hunter*.

Christopher Reeve stars in *Superman*.

The Village People release *YMCA* and *In the Navy*.

Evita opens in London.

Taxi appears on U.S. TV.

Mork and Mindy appears on U.S. TV.

Dallas appears on U.S. TV.

Norman Rockwell dies.

1979

Corvette equipment now includes stereo, adjustable steering column, and power windows and door locks in the base price. The Corvette's base price is now $12,313. Sales exceed 50,000.

The price of oil doubles due to revolution in Iran.

The Chrysler Corporation requires financial assistance from the federal government to save it from bankruptcy.

Margaret Thatcher becomes Britain's first woman prime minister.

Ayatollah Khomeini becomes leader in Iran.

The U.S. embassy in Tripoli, Libya, is burned.

Soviet troops invade Afghanistan.

The Rubik's Cube goes on sale in the U.S.

The Post-it sticker goes on sale in the U.S.

The Sony Walkman goes on sale in the U.S.

Ridley Scott's *Alien* is released.

Francis Ford Coppola's *Apocalypse Now* is released.

Peter Sellers stars in *Being There*.

Mel Gibson stars in *Mad Max*.

The Dukes of Hazzard appears on U.S. TV.

Hart to Hart appears on U.S. TV.

Rick Mears wins the first Champion Auto Racing Teams (CART) World Series.

Fuzzy Zoeller wins the Masters golf tournament in his first attempt.

Sid Vicious and Mary Pickford die.

1980

The Corvette sheds 150 lb., largely through the use of aluminum parts in place of steel. The spoilers from the Indy pace car replica are incorporated into the nose and tail to improve aerodynamics. Production drops by over 13,000.

The General Motors Corporation declares a loss for the first time since 1921.

The Iran–Iraq war breaks out.

IBM develops a voice-recognition system that can display words on the computer screen at the speed at which they are spoken.

Carl Sagan publishes *Cosmos*.

Tom Wolfe publishes *The Right Stuff*.

Stanley Kubrick's *The Shining* is released.

Martin Scorsese's *Raging Bull* is released.

John Landis's *The Blues Brothers* is released.

Irvin Kershner's *The Empire Strikes Back* is released.

Cable News Network (CNN) goes on air, 24 hours a day.

Dallas breaks all existing ratings when the "Who shot J. R.?" episode is broadcast on television and watched by over 114 million people.

Twenty-three-year-old Seve Ballesteros becomes the youngest winner of the Masters golf tournament.

Johnny Rutherford wins his third Indy 500.

Mae West and Peters Sellers die.

John Lennon is murdered in New York.

1981

Corvette sales steady at around 40,600. Weight-saving measures continue with the literal "slimming down" of GRP body panels and window glass. A fiberglass rear leaf spring is adopted. A new version of the 350 cu. in. small-block is introduced; the L81 uses a computer-controlled engine management system.

Ronald Reagan is sworn in as 40th President of the United States.

Iran releases 52 U.S. hostages they have held for over a year.

President Reagan is wounded in an assassination attempt.

Pope John Paul II is wounded in an assassination attempt.

IBM launches their first PC using the Microsoft MS-DOS operating system.

The FDA approves Nutrasweet.

The U.S. government lends the Chrysler Corporation $400 million.

Striking U.S. air-traffic controllers are fired when they refuse to return to work.

MTV goes on air for the first time.

John Boorman's *Excalibur* is released.

Steven Spielberg's *Raiders of the Lost Ark* is released.

Charles, Prince of Wales, marries Lady Diana Spencer.

Dynasty appears on U.S. TV.

Driver Richard Petty wins the Daytona 500 for the seventh time.

Jockey Bill Shoemaker rides his 8,000th winner.

Joe Louis and Bob Marley die.

1982

Corvette production has now been relocated to an exclusive, purpose-built facility at Bowling Green, Kentucky. A new model from the new factory is keenly anticipated. Sales slip to a ten-year low of 25,407. Japanese cars now account for nearly a quarter of the U.S. market.

The DeLorean car factory in Northern Ireland closes.

Apple Computers achieves sales of a billion dollars.

Argentina invades the British colony of the Falkland Islands, and British troops expel the invaders. Casualties: 255 British, 652 Argentine.

The Vietnam War Memorial in Washington is unveiled. It lists the names of over 58,000 U.S. service personnel killed or missing.

Kodak produces the first digital camera.

Sony produces the first CD player.

Graceland opens to the public in Memphis, Tennessee.

EPCOT opens to the public in Lake Buena Vista, Florida.

Arnold Schwarzenegger stars in *Conan the Barbarian*.

Dustin Hoffman stars in *Tootsie*.

Michael Jackson's *Thriller* is the best-selling album of all time.

Madonna appears on MTV for the first time.

USA Today appears on U.S. newsstands for the first time.

Cheers appears on U.S. TV for the first time.

The first bicycle Race Across America is won by Lon Haldeman, covering nearly 3,000 miles in just under ten days.

John Belushi and Grace Kelly die.

1984

A fourth-generation Corvette, built on a "backbone" chassis, with completely new running gear, is released. Powered by the L83 incarnation of the 350 small-block, with "Cross-Fire" fuel injection, it is more aerodynamically efficient and roomier than its predecessor.

Over seventy American banks collapse.

Arab terrorists attack the U.S. embassy in Beirut.

Irish terrorists attack the Grand Hotel in Brighton, England, where the prime minister, Margaret Thatcher, is staying.

Apple launches the Macintosh personal computer.

The CD-ROM is introduced.

Union Carbide pays nearly half a billion dollars in damages when a chemical leak at their factory in Bhopal, India, kills more than 2,500 people.

San Francisco bathhouses are closed in an attempt to halt the spread of the AIDS virus among the gay community.

Miami Vice appears on U.S. TV.

Bruce Springsteen releases *Born in the U.S.A.*

Madonna releases *Like a Virgin.*

Harrison Ford stars in *Indiana Jones and the Temple of Doom.*

Arnold Schwarzenegger stars in *The Terminator.*

Rick Mears wins the Indy 500.

Laurent Fignon wins the Tour de France.

Marvin Gaye dies.

Prince Harry is born.

1985

The complex, fuel-saving, "4 + 3" gearbox designed by Doug Nash proves controversial. Fuel injection is changed from "Cross-Fire" to "Tuned-Port" and 25 bhp is gained. Suspension is revised for improved ride.

Soviet leader Mikhail Gorbachev announces the need for *glasnost* (transparency) in government policy.

President Reagan announces increased spending on the so-called Star Wars defense system to $26,000,000,000.

The IRS uses computers to process tax returns for the first time.

A hole in Earth's ozone layer is detected above Antarctica.

The Greenpeace vessel *Rainbow Warrior* is blown up by French secret agents while anchored in New Zealand.

Palestinian hijackers seize the Italian cruise ship *Achille Lauro.*

The wreck of the *Titanic* is discovered.

A DeLorean appears in Robert Zemeckis's *Back to the Future.*

John Lennon's Rolls Royce is sold for three million dollars.

Live Aid concerts raise over seventy million dollars to feed the starving in Africa.

Pictures of missing children appear on U.S. milk cartons.

The Golden Girls appears on U.S. TV.

Danny Sullivan wins the Indy 500.

Bernard Hinault wins the Tour de France.

Clarence Nash, voice of Donald Duck for nearly fifty years, dies.

Orson Welles dies.

1986

The roadster returns. After a decade's absence, a fully convertible Corvette is offered once more. Bosch antilock brakes are fitted as standard equipment. The L98 small-block gets aluminum cylinder heads and a higher compression ratio.

General Motors is once more the richest company in the United States.

Wall Street suffers the worst fall in share prices since the crash of 1929.

A Russian nuclear power plant at Chernobyl explodes.

A plant for irradiating fruit is opened in New Jersey.

Nintendo launches "Super Mario Brothers."

Garrison Keillor publishes *Lake Wobegon Days*.

Tom Cruise stars in *Top Gun*.

Sigourney Weaver stars in *Aliens*.

Paul Simon releases *Graceland*.

Run-DMC releases *Raisin' Hell*.

Willie Shoemaker (54) becomes the oldest jockey to win the Kentucky Derby.

Ray Floyd (43) becomes the oldest golfer to win the U.S. Open.

Mike Tyson (20) becomes the youngest boxer to win the WBC heavyweight title.

Greg Lemond becomes the first American cyclist to win the Tour de France.

Oliver North is fired.

Otto Preminger dies.

1987

Roller valve lifters help to push the Corvette's power output to 240 bhp. Sales hover around 30,000, of which about a third are convertibles. Base prices are now $27,999 for the coupe and $33,172 for the roadster.

On "Black Monday" (Oct. 19) the Dow Jones index falls by over five hundred points, almost a quarter of its value.

The U.S. dollar is at an all-time low on world currency markets.

An Iraqi missile strikes the *USS Stark*, on patrol in the Persian Gulf.

A German teenager lands a microlight aircraft in Moscow's Red Square.

The FDA approves AZT as a treatment for AIDS.

The FDA approves Prozac as a treatment for depression.

Margaret Thatcher is elected British prime minister for the third time.

Stanley Kubrick's *Full Metal Jacket* is released.

Barry Levinson's *Good Morning, Vietnam* is released.

Michael Douglas and Glenn Close star in *Fatal Attraction*.

Michael Douglas and Charlie Sheen star in *Wall Street*.

Tom Wolfe publishes *Bonfire of the Vanities*.

Irish cyclist Stephen Roche emulates Eddy Merckx by winning the Tour de France, the Giro d'Italia, and the World Road Race Championship in the same year.

U.S. basketball player Michael Jordan emulates Wilt Chamberlain by scoring 3,000 points in a season.

Liberace and Andy Warhol die.

1988

Having missed out on a thirtieth birthday party, the Corvette celebrated its thirty-fifth with a limited-edition anniversary model. Suspension was improved on all cars to reduce dive and squat, underbraking, and acceleration.

The U.S. national debt exceeds a trillion dollars ($1,000,000,000,000).

Wall Street suffers the largest single-day loss in its history.

McDonald's opens its 10,000th outlet.

George Bush is nominated by the Republican Party.

A Pan American Boeing 747 is destroyed by an explosion over the Scottish town of Lockerbie. 259 passengers and crew are killed, plus eleven people on the ground.

The *USS Vincennes* shoots down an Iranian airlines plane over the Persian Gulf. 286 passengers and crew are killed.

Dustin Hoffman and Tom Cruise star in *Rain Man*.

Gene Hackman and Willem Dafoe star in *Mississippi Burning*.

Robert Zemeckis's *Who Framed Roger Rabbit?* is released.

Thomas Harris publishes *The Silence of the Lambs*.

Stephen Hawking publishes *A Brief History of Time*.

Roseanne appears on U.S. TV.

War and Remembrance appears on U.S. TV.

Rick Mears wins the Indy 500.

Felix Wankel and Enzo Ferrari die.

1989

Total production approaches 900,000. Six-speed, manual transmission is introduced, along with Selective Ride Control. The Z53 suspension package, with 17-inch wheels and tires, becomes standard equipment. A $2,000 detachable hardtop for the convertible is made available.

George Bush is sworn in as 41st President of the United States.

The Dow Jones index falls nearly 200 points.

The French celebrate the bicentennial of their revolution.

The Germans celebrate the dismantling of the Berlin Wall.

The Exxon *Valdez* spills nine million gallons of oil in Prince William Sound, Alaska.

Sony buys Columbia Pictures.

Mitsubishi buys Rockefeller Center.

Panama declares war on the United States.

The United States invades Panama.

Oliver North goes on trial for shredding documents.

Zsa Zsa Gabor goes to jail for slapping a traffic cop.

Michael Keaton stars in *Batman*.

Jessica Tandy stars in *Driving Miss Daisy*.

Lonesome Dove is shown on U.S. TV.

American Greg Lemond wins the Tour de France by the narrowest margin ever.

America qualifies for the soccer World Cup for the first time since 1950.

Emperor Hirohito of Japan and Ayatollah Khomeini die.

1990

The ZR1 appears. With near race car specifications, it is the most expensive automobile ever produced by General Motors, retailing at $59,000. The Lotus-developed, all-alloy, four-cam, thirty-two valve, 375 bhp engine provides a top speed of over 170 mph and a 0–60 time of 4.5 seconds.

Nelson Mandela is released after over twenty-five years of imprisonment in South Africa.

Mikhail Gorbachev is awarded the Nobel Prize for Peace.

Iraqi troops invade Kuwait.

U.S. and allied forces engage Iraq in Operation Desert Storm.

Margaret Thatcher resigns as British prime minister and is succeeded by John Major.

Kevin Costner directs and stars in *Dances with Wolves*.

Martin Scorsese coscripts and directs *GoodFellas*.

Macauley Culkin stars in *Home Alone*.

Johnny Depp stars in *Edward Scissorhands*.

M. C. Hammer releases *Please Hammer Don't Hurt 'Em*.

Chris Rea releases *Road to Hell*.

Twin Peaks appears on U.S. TV.

The Simpsons appears on U.S. TV.

Magic Johnson of the L.A. Lakers is named the NBA's most valuable player for the third time.

Greg Lemond wins the Tour de France for the third time.

McDonald's opens an outlet in Moscow.

Greta Garbo dies.

1991

The fourth-generation Corvettes, including the "King of the Hill" ZR1 are subtly restyled. To the annoyance of many who had paid over even the astronomic list price of the ZR1, standard 'Vettes got identical rear-end treatment, right down to the squared-off taillights. To add insult to injury, by midyear ZR1 prices are being discounted.

Nelson Mandela becomes president of the African National Congress.

Pan Am files for bankruptcy.

The Bank of Credit and Commerce collapses.

U.S. and allied forces expel Iraqi forces from Kuwait.

George Bush and Mikhail Gorbachev agree on a Strategic Arms Reduction Treaty (SALT) to reduce their nuclear weapons stocks by a third.

Sony launches the minidisk.

Sega Games introduces "Sonic the Hedgehog."

The first Planet Hollywood restaurant opens in New York.

Kevin Costner stars in *JFK*.

Nirvana releases *Nevermind*.

Michael Jackson releases *Dangerous*.

Jeff Gordon wins the Daytona 500 in a Chevrolet.

Rick Mears wins the Indy 500 for the fourth time.

The New York Giants beat the Buffalo Bills 20-19 in the Super Bowl.

Freddy Mercury and Dr. Seuss die.

2000

A special millennium edition is produced, in striking Millennium Yellow. This recalls the C5R racing Corvettes that were enjoying increasing success in endurance racing at Sebring, Daytona, and in the Le Mans 24-hour race. The wheel spokes are slimmed down and interior trim is revised and improved.

Smith & Wesson limit the manufacture and distribution of handguns.

South Carolina removes the Confederate flag from its capitol dome.

The "I love you" virus causes worldwide disruption to computer systems.

Dale Jarrett wins the Daytona 500.

Venus Williams wins the Wimbledon and U.S. Open tennis championships and a gold medal at the Sydney Olympic Games.

Tiger Woods wins the PGA Championship.

Michael Schumacher wins the Formula One world championship.

Lance Armstrong wins the Tour de France.

Gladiator is released.

Cast Away is released.

Scary Movie is released.

The Beatles release "1."

U2 releases *All that You Can't Leave Behind*.

Madonna releases *Music*.

Charles Schultz and Patrick O'Brian die.

Hedy Lamarr dies.

2001

A new Z06 is introduced as an option on the hardtop. The new LS6 engine is rated at 385 bhp—more powerful than the first-generation ZR1s. The Z06 has practical vents for rear brake cooling, red-colored brake calipers, and signature wheels fitted with run-flat Goodyear Eagle Supercar tires.

George W. Bush is sworn in as 43rd President of the United States.

Terrorists fly two airliners into the twin towers of the World Trade Center in New York and one into the Pentagon in Washington, D.C. A fourth plane comes down outside Pittsburgh.

The Taliban regime in Afghanistan collapses after a sustained attack by U.S. and allied forces.

Harlem Globetrotters Meadowlark Lemon (#36) and Marques Haynes (#20) join Wilt Chamberlain (#13) in the distinction of having their numbers retired by the team.

Dale Earnhardt is killed on the last lap of the Daytona 500. Michael Waltrip wins.

Dale Earnhardt Jr. crashes on the first lap of the DuraLube 400 but is uninjured.

Michael Schumacher wins the Formula One world championship.

Lance Armstrong wins the Tour de France.

Harry Potter and the Sorcerer's Stone is released.

The Lord of the Rings: The Fellowship of the Ring is released.

Bob Dylan releases *Love and Theft*.

Alicia Keys releases *Songs in A-Minor*.

Anthony Quinn dies.

Larry Adler dies.

2002

Z06 output is increased to a staggering 405 bhp, making it by far the most powerful 350 ever. All Corvettes now cost over $40,000. The Corvette is chosen to pace the Indy 500 for the fifth time. Three pace car replicas are produced, but they are not for sale.

The U.S. incarcerates prisoners of war from the campaign in Afghanistan in Guantanamo Bay, Cuba.

U.S. reporter Daniel Pearl is murdered in Pakistan.

The U.S. Justice Department opens a criminal investigation into collapsed energy company Enron Corp.

Horror writer Stephen King announces his retirement.

Queen Elizabeth II of England celebrates her golden jubilee.

Queen Elizabeth, the Queen Mother, dies at 101.

WorldCom files for bankruptcy.

Ward Burton wins the Daytona 500.

Sprinter Tim Montgomery becomes the fastest man on earth, covering 100 meters in 9.78 seconds.

Martin Buser wins the Iditarod Sled Dog Race for the fourth time.

Lance Armstrong wins the Tour de France for the fourth time.

Star Wars Episode II: The Attack of the Clones is released.

The Lord of the Rings: The Two Towers is released.

Blind Boys of Alabama release *Higher Ground*.

Bruce Springsteen and the E Street Band release *The Rising*.

Billy Wilder and James Coburn die.

Ann Landers, advice columnist, dies.

2003

Corvette's 50th anniversary is marked by a special edition. The anniversary model is available in a special Anniversary Red with champagne-tinted wheels and two-tone shale interior. The new F55 Selective Magnetic Ride control is fitted to all anniversary models. This system allows the car's ride to be monitored and adjusted every half an inch traveled at sixty miles per hour.

North Korea withdraws from treaty on the nonproliferation of nuclear weapons.

Ariel Sharon elected Israeli prime minister.

Space shuttle *Columbia* explodes, killing all seven astronauts.

The United States and Britain launch war against Iraq and Baghdad falls to U.S. troops.

Saddam Hussein is arrested by U.S. troops.

Roman Polanski wins the Academy Award for Best Director for his movie *The Pianist*.

Beyonce releases *Crazy in Love*.

The White Stripes release *Seven Army Nation*.

Harley-Davidson celebrates its 100th anniversary in Milwaukee with a parade of 10,000 motorcycles.

Actor Alan Bates dies.

Bob Hope (100), master of the one-liner and favorite comedian of servicemen and presidents alike, dies at his home in Toluca Lake.

2004

The final year of the C5 Corvette sees a commemorative edition Z06 to mark Le Mans victories in 2001 and 2002 and a sixth Indy 500 pace car.

Bush wins another term as President, overcoming opposition from Democrat leader John Kerry.

The world's most powerful earthquake in 40 years triggers massive tidal waves that slam into villages and seaside resorts across southern and southeast Asia killing thousands.

Ninety gay and lesbian couples wed in San Francisco. Over the next few days some 2,000 take their vows.

Entertainer Janet Jackson covered her breast after singer Justin Timberlake ripped off one of her chest plates during the halftime Super Bowl performance in Houston, Texas.

The Academy Award for Best Picture goes to *Lord of the Rings: The Return of the King*.

The final episode of TV show *Sex and the City* aired after a 6-season run.

Lance Armstrong wins his sixth Tour de France in succession.

American swimming sensation Michael Phelps finishes the Athens Olympic Games with six gold and two bronze, the eight medals tying the single Games record.

Michael Schumacher wins a record seventh Formula One Championship title.

Palestinian leader Yasser Arafat dies.

Singer Ray Charles dies.

2005

The C6 Corvette debuts, showing exposed headlights for the first time since 1962, and sets new standards in performance, ride, handling, and fuel efficiency that others will find hard to equal—at any price.

George W. Bush sworn in for a second term as President of the United States.

Democratic elections held in Afghanistan and Iraq.

Jeff Weise, 16, shoots and kills his grandfather, five teenagers, a teacher, and two other adults before turning the gun on himself, in Red Lake, Minnesota.

Michael Jackson trial commences.

Ray Charles is a awarded posthumous Grammy for *Genius Loves Company*.

Clint Eastwood takes Best Picture and Best Director Academy Awards for *Million Dollar Baby*.

Hunter S. Thompson, author of *Fear and Loathing in Las Vegas*, commits suicide.

John DeLorean, creator of the futuristic sportscar of the 1980s, dies.

Index